# ACCELERATE
## *your*
# CAREER

# PRAISE FOR OTHER BOOKS BY DOROTHY TANNAHILL-MORAN

*"I've read countless books on small talk, body language and managing contacts. But none of these books really addressed the elephant in the room, my social reluctance. Until now! As a social media guy, I particularly like the call-outs to Twitter, Facebook and LinkedIn. These tools are absent in most other networking books. Three cheers!"*

### Joshua Waldman
AUTHOR, "JOB SEARCHING WITH SOCIAL MEDIA FOR DUMMIES"

*"Written for people who see themselves as introverts or socially reluctant, PERSONAL BRANDING makes an intelligent contribution to the discussion of networking, an activity of dramatically increasing importance for personal stability in an increasingly uncertain professional world."*

### Martin Yate, CPC
NEW YORK TIMES BEST-SELLING AUTHOR,
"KNOCK EM DEAD—SECRETS & STRATEGIES FOR SUCCESS IN AN UNCERTAIN WORLD"

*"Dorothy Tannahill Moran hits the nail on the head in her book, ELEVATOR SPEECHES THAT GET RESULTS. In this quick, easy read, I gained a deeper appreciation for the Elevator Speech as a tool for managing my personal brand. This little gem not only offers suggestions for how to use a well-crafted Elevator Speech, but also provides helpful tips for creating one, if not several. I especially appreciated her insight into what works and doesn't work in creating and delivering an Elevator Speech and have been inspired to rewrite my own. Well done!"*

### Kristen Clark
CONFIDENCE COACH, AWARD-WINNING AUTHOR, EDITOR, PUBLISHER

*"Dorothy delivers smart, actionable advice that gets results.. CAREER MAPPING is imperative—now more than ever—for anyone looking to accelerate professionally and maintain more control in this rapidly changing economy. The book is a "must read."*

### Kevin M. Kermes
FOUNDER, ALL THINGS CAREER

**the publishing CIRCLE**

admin@ThePublishingCircle.com
or
THE PUBLISHING CIRCLE
Regarding: Dorothy Tannahill-Moran
19215 SE 34th Street
Suite 106-347
Camas, Washington 98607

ACCELERATE YOUR CAREER EVEN WITH A BAD BOSS:
A NEW APPROACH TO MANAGING UP / DOROTHY TANNAHILL-MORAN
ISBN 978-1-947398-07-8

*Book design by Michele Uplinger*

# ACCELERATE
## *your*
# CAREER

## EVEN WITH
## A BAD BOSS

*A New Approach
to Managing Up*

Get Free Instant Access to Video series,

## "The 5 Most Common Ways
## Introverts Commit Career Self-Sabotage
## and How to Avoid Them"

These videos are designed to accelerate your results
with **Accelerate Your Career,**
and are my way of saying "thank you" for purchasing this book.

www.introvertwhisperer.com/career goals

# Contents

Foreword . . . . . . . . . . . . . . . . . . . . . . . . . . ix

Introduction . . . . . . . . . . . . . . . . . . . . . 3

Bad Boss Story #1 . . . . . . . . . . . . . . . . . 7

Self-Management:
Empowerment & Intimidation . . . . . . . . . . . 11

Is It You? Perspectives From the Boss . . . . . . . 19

Things You Can & Should Do
to Manage Your Performance . . . . . . . . . . . 25

Seek Performance Feedback on Ongoing Basis. . . 29

Bad Boss Story #2 . . . . . . . . . . . . . . . . . . 35

Managing "Up" . . . . . . . . . . . . . . . . . . . . 39

Bad Boss Story #3 . . . . . . . . . . . . . . . . . . 63

Managing Your Bad Boss . . . . . . . . . . . . . 567

Types of Bad Bosses . . . . . . . . . . . . . . . . . 73

Bad Boss Story #4 . . . . . . . . . . . . . . . . . . 91

You Hired *Who* To Be My Boss? . . . . . . . . . 95

Bad Boss Story #5 . . . . . . . . . . . . . . . . . 115

More Bad Boss Stories . . . . . . . . . . . . . . 119

Final Thoughts . . . . . . . . . . . . . . . . . . . 135

About the Author . . . . . . . . . . . . . . . . . 140

# FOREWORD

I HAVE YET TO MEET a person who doesn't have a Bad Boss story to tell. It's an unfortunate fact of working life. Our enlightened modern-day societies, along with massive amounts of laws that govern employment, have largely done away with the most exploitive management behavior. I say "mostly", because you don't have to dig too far to find some of the most egregious Bad Boss behaviors still alive and well.

My own career path launched me into the arms of a notoriously Bad Boss at the ripe old age of seventeen. It was my first job and I was still in high school. I was in a work-study program and working was a requirement. I never thought I had an option to quit, so I quickly learned some strategies that helped me survive. Little did I know that what I learned working for that Bad Boss helped condition me for a career full of poor behaving, stupid, and ego-fueled managers. The good news is that I discovered how to deal with each Bad Boss in ways that served my clients and me well.

I have to give you some insight into my first boss. She was about seventy years old and the owner of the biggest and best fabric shop in our city. In the time I worked for her, I witnessed a new hire quit after one hour on the job. This person was an adult. Another co-worker was brought to tears in front of a customer (which as a seventeen-year-old stunned me because I couldn't fathom that an adult would have this kind of behavior aimed at them). The customer was openly cringing and kept assuring the boss that everything was good for her. The bad boss ignored the customer to continue her tirade.

I saw my Bad Boss throw a fit and pull down a wall of fabric bolts, only to yell at the workers to pick it all up. Her policy was that you were never to speak to other co-workers, as none of them knew as much as she did. If you had questions, you were to ask only her—and she wasn't around but about half the time. She loved to show up unexpectedly so she could catch someone doing something she didn't like. That would allow her to yell at them and ride them around the store relentlessly for as much as 15–30 minutes in a non-stop rant.

One time when I disagreed with her, she went into a rage and starting yelling. For some reason, I walked away so I didn't have to listen, which only enraged her more. To stop me, she grabbed me, spun me around, and started shaking me like a rag doll. I pulled my arms away from her and told her she didn't have permission to touch me. She was stunned into silence. "You can yell at me. That's your right to do so, but it is my right to stop listening. You are never to touch me again."

That instance and the others I've mentioned were just some of the "highlights." I worked there for a year until I moved to go to college. I didn't get fired and I didn't leave in tears.

When I left, I vowed to be the best possible manager

and leader I could be. I would learn there are a huge percentage of managers and leaders who are bad in all sorts of ways.

It didn't take long to also discover that your boss and your perception of them is THE single biggest factor for how well you like your job. Most people think it's the paycheck, but if you think about it for a few minutes, you'll realize it's true. If you have a despicable person to work for, there is almost no amount of money that will make that be okay, nor will it make it acceptable. Knowing how impactful management is on the daily satisfaction of the people in their charge fueled me to not only be the best boss, but to produce the best management possible.

I should also point out that the majority of people in a leadership role don't fall into the Bad Boss category.

I do know that when your boss *is* bad, it can overtake your life, creating stress and extreme unhappiness. The Bad Boss situation happens too often, and my goal is to give you strategies that will reduce the effects and even improve your situation.

Get Free Instant Access to Video series,

## "The 5 Most Common Ways Introverts Commit Career Self-Sabotage and How to Avoid Them"

These videos are designed to accelerate your results
with **Accelerate Your Career,**
and are my way of saying "thank you" for purchasing this book.

www.introvertwhisperer.com/career goals

THE INTROVERT
WHISPERER™

# ACCELERATE
## *your*
# CAREER

## EVEN WITH
## A BAD BOSS

*A New Approach
to Managing Up*

DOROTHY TANNAHILL-MORAN

# INTRODUCTION TO ACCELERATE YOUR CAREER— EVEN WITH A BAD BOSS

## WHAT WE WILL COVER AND WHY

THERE IS AN ENTIRE industry dedicated solely to the improvement and skill-development of leaders and managers. If you surf through a bookstore, you can find literally thousands of books on how to manage. Seminar companies exist solely to teach management skills. There are thousands of management consulting companies, countless management and executive coaches, not to mention in-house HR types dedicated to keeping the company and leaders out of court. Get the drift? The fact that an entire industry exists because leadership is so impactful is almost proof enough that a problem exists. Poor management is pervasive.

We're having an epidemic of soul-sucking people out there in the workplace. Because most of us must work for a living, the only option seems to be to put up with the abuse.

While our management-makeover industry is largely losing, my tactic here is to help wage a good offense for you. Like all bad behavior, I think you have to figure out what the bad behavior is and try to be as effective as you can be to work with it. You would be wrong to think you can change someone else's bad behavior—you can't change someone else (even your spouse or partner) and you shouldn't even think you can change the boss. You would also be wasting your energy to hope this bad boss will somehow wake up and magically be transformed into a loving visionary.

So, is this book a dyspeptic review of bad behavior? No, it's an acknowledgement that while you will periodically have a Bad Boss, there are things you can do to manage yourself and the situation. This is a form of "managing up" and also a form of self-management. You must take responsibility for working effectively with others, no matter who they are. By doing so, you empower yourself and take ownership of your career. You can optimize your Bad Boss.

What I will cover in this book is a comprehensive review of actions you can take to cover most of the circumstances surrounding you and your Bad Boss. We will start by looking at some aspects of your own self-management and empowerment.

From there, we will cover an array of behaviors employees have that can "set off" even a fairly reasonable manager. Again, these are things you have control over as long as you choose to internalize the message and examine your actions to see if you may be doing things to make your situation worse.

We will cover the essential elements of Managing Up. This is a set of practices you will want to adopt as long as you work for someone else. Many of the tenets of Managing Up form the framework for *Accelerate Your Career—Even with a Bad Boss*. Managing Up will make a good manager into a saint, and a Bad Boss acceptable.

We will then look at a selection of Bad Boss types and actions you can take to mitigate the negative effects. It's impossible to cover all the possible ways a boss can be bad, but the profiles I have covered are the most common ways.

I have also included a collection of Bad Boss stories to both entertain and provide some additional insights, should you experience a similar person. I very carefully ensured that the information presented in these stories, while true, is scrubbed of any distinguishing information about the guilty.

At the end of the book, I have covered an array of situations that may come your way at some point in your career, depending on the person managing you. It's good for you to know how to manage under a variety of circumstances. I think the best thing I cover is the perennial question: "How did this person get the job?"

It will get better.

# BAD BOSS STORY #1

I SHARE THIS STORY mostly to illustrate my point about egregious behavior. It's one of the worst Bad Boss stories I've heard. I spoke to the man who told me this story at a networking event. All I had to do was ask: Who was the worst Bad Boss you've had? Here is his response:

"I suddenly had a health crisis in the early morning hours a couple of years ago. It was so bad I had to call for an ambulance to take me to the hospital. After being in the emergency room and going through a battery of tests, it became apparent I wasn't going to make it to work. I called my boss on his cell phone to let him know I wasn't going to be at work and that I was in an emergency room. His reaction? He insisted I get to work and stop the nonsense. I couldn't believe what he said, so I repeated that I was in no condition to go to work. He didn't care what my excuse was, he said, I was to head to work immediately. Seeing I wasn't going to get anywhere with him, I told him I'd call him later to let him know if I was going to be admitted to the hospital and when I would return to work. I thought that was it.

Apparently, my boss was enraged. He drove straight to the hospital. He made his way into the emergency room and found me lying there with IVs and monitors hooked up. Despite that, he began yelling at me to get up and get dressed immediately and get to work. The nurses tried to calm him down and make him leave, but he didn't respond to them. Additional people on the ER staff tried to defuse the situation. Finally, hospital security was called to escort him out of the hospital.

I was admitted to the hospital and released the next day. I wasn't sure what to do, so I simply showed up for work and resumed working. The boss didn't say a thing about what had taken place or fire me, so I stuck with the job for a while.

## My thoughts on this Bad Boss:

While I'm a believer that you can reduce the effects of a Bad Boss with good Managing Up skills, nothing could have prevented this. It's possible this Bad Boss suffers from mental health issues, as the behavior is so unbalanced. Nevertheless, this incident would completely eliminate any trust and permanently damage the relationship for the employee going forward.

I do applaud this man for simply showing up to work instead of crawling away to avoid the boss or making assumptions about his employment status.

# SELF-MANAGEMENT
*Make Sure YOU Aren't
the Cause of a Bad Boss*

## EMPOWERMENT AND INTIMIDATION

### Self-Empowerment

BEFORE GETTING INTO the specifics, I think it's important to acknowledge that YOU are most likely going to be changing some behaviors. While I do detail steps you can take, you must feel a sense of self-empowerment to act on what you learn. Instruction without action is philosophy. If you do not empower yourself, you are never going to improve your Bad Boss situation. You will remain unhappy and eventually start feeling like a victim, which will only make your future bleak.

Understand that no one will, or can, do any of the things I outline here but you. The good news for the person who is fearful or seriously reluctant is that it only takes one small step. You are building a skill and the place to start is with one or two things of the many things I outline. You can and should start doing those things today. Once you master that, you can build on these skills and try more of them. The person who is empowered is simply using a set of skills they have developed and mastered. Each small victory builds the confidence and thus, your own empowerment. This may sound simplistic. It is. I think some people try to make power and empowerment out to be this esoteric and mysterious "state-of-being." Self-empowerment is simply your confidence based on the execution of what you learn. It's *you* giving *yourself* permission to take action.

The last thing I also want to point out is that you should never be in too much awe of another person—especially your boss. Your job is to respect them and acknowledge their role in your place of business. It's the same thing you want for yourself. A boss, simply because of their position, intimidates all too many people. When you are intimidated by anyone, you give your power away and actually set yourself up to be abused. You must remember that the boss is human just like you and at one time had lower-level jobs. They have to go home and put out the trash and deal with the same messiness of life. They have many of the same motivations in life as you. The only difference is they have a different job than yours and have their own unique personality.

## Intimidation

If you allow yourself to be intimidated by another person, you are doing more damage than you might imagine. As I mentioned previously, you must empower yourself to take action. No one else can do for you what you must do in a bad situation.

When another person intimidates you, it shows. You may not think it does, especially if you keep that information to yourself, but it does show. When I was a high-level manager it only took me a couple of seconds to recognize when a person was intimidated by me. And trust me, I'm not really an intimidating person, but apparently the position I was in did cause some people to be intimidated. Everyone can see a lack of confidence or intimidation in others. Body language gives that away, as does how a person chooses to speak.

Unfortunately, as humans we have an almost primal instinct to abuse a weak person. My personal analysis is that it has to do with our innate survival instincts. If one person in the tribe is unable to defend, it opens us all to danger. In modern terms, we aren't exposed to as many threats in our environment but the lingering urge to eliminate weakness or toughen it up remains.

This means if you give your power away by being intimidated by the Bad Boss, you are opening up the situation to potentially get worse than it might otherwise be.

I once worked for a man who could bring both men and women in the group to tears. My direct manager worked for him and they seemed to work well together. I never understood why he had such a different effect with different people until I was promoted and started working for him. It wasn't long before he and I got into some fairly big confrontations. These weren't limited to in-person interactions, as we had a couple of big ones while I was traveling and using the phone with him. The one thing I noticed is that after all was said and done between us, he usually agreed with me and was supportive. Very odd.

One day I figured it out and when I did, I shared my observations with him. He would always test you on your decisions and directions by taking an opposite argument. If you gave in to him, he got viscous and unrelenting. If you stood up to him, he respected you. When I shared this with him, his laughter roared throughout the building. I had hit the truth! He told me no one had ever really figured this out or at least never shared with him that they understood what he was doing. He explained it was his nature, but he felt you should always be able to stand and defend your decisions. Those were the only type of people he wanted to work with or would ever respect. He loved the fact that I had figured it out.

Did that mean he backed down to me once I knew his secret? No. We argued frequently.

I share this story to not only illustrate how I dealt with this boss but to also illustrate an important point. If you give away your power, if you allow yourself to be intimidated by someone, you open yourself up to further abuse and a lack of respect. You will only make your Bad Boss worse.

If you're prone to allowing yourself to be intimidated, you may think there is nothing you can do other than go with your natural reactions. This is not the case. You have to realize that somewhere in your life, you were taught to react this way. This means you can learn a new way to react to others. It does take a certain amount of discipline, but it can be done.   You have to first identify specific things you are reacting to. It may be any or all of the following:

- A person's position

- A person's perceived status, i.e. wealthy, important, etc.

- How a person interacts with you or others

- A person's perceived leverage over you

Once you understand what might trigger your sense of intimidation, you can define a course of action to take under similar situations. Here are some suggestions, but don't limit your thoughts to only these:

1. If a person's position in management causes you to be intimidated, you can remember that this person had to come up through the ranks just

like you. You can tell yourself that this person simply wants the business to be successful and is still a person with the same type of dreams as you. Create a picture in your mind of a "normal person." This applies to anyone, no matter if they are wealthy, important, or an executive.

2. If a person interacts with you or others in a way that intimidates you, spend time observing these interactions as objectively as possible. Do not put extra meaning into their words or actions. Ask yourself, what ways could you interpret what they are doing? Most of the time, people who intimidate others may simply have a more brusque way of tackling problems and use poor social skills in the process. They may have the best of intentions. Consider that you may have read more into their actions than was their intent. Create a different, more positive way of seeing their behavior.

The more you do this sort of mental exercise, the more it will become second nature. It's like any exercise. The more you work a muscle group, the stronger that muscle becomes. The same thing applies to mental muscles. You have to remember you are *choosing* how you are going to react to another person. Do you *choose* to be intimidated, or will you choose to see the other person as human, just like you?

I had a manager in my group who was a superb expert in our line of work. His work was close to flawless. He was, however, not one for the extra social "nice-ities" like greeting everyone in the morning and shooting the breeze. He was focused and got a lot of work done. Increasingly, I had more and more people in this group complain about him being a Bad Boss. He and I spoke about it but were at a loss about what was at the root of the issue.

I eventually sat down with the primary complainers and got to the root cause of their issues with him. It wasn't that he was "bad" per se. But because he didn't choose to socially interact very much and could spot problems seriously fast, they were intimidated by his obvious perfection. Matters were made worse because of the lack of relationships with members of the group.

In other words, these people were making a choice about how they felt when they were around this manager. It didn't matter that he didn't harbor any beliefs that they had to know as much as he did. In fact, he openly shared his knowledge, but only when asked. It also never occurred to him that saying "good morning" to people was important, because it wasn't important him.

My remedy was with both the manager and the rest of the team. His employees had to take responsibility for social interactions and build a relationship with this manager. I counseled his employees on how they were making a choice about how they viewed him. At the same time, I worked with the manager to help him become more deliberate about his social interactions and more forthcoming with knowledge transfer. The situation turned around quickly, and everyone became satisfied with their interactions.

# IS IT YOU?

*Is the Boss Really Being Difficult,*
*or Is It You?*

## PERSPECTIVES FROM THE BOSS

I N AN HR-ORIENTED Linked-In group, someone posted a discussion that well over 2,400 people commented on. The flavor of the discussion was: *Why is it so hard to find good employees?* And here we are in a book about Bad Bosses, so I'm sure there is a similar discussion in another group on that topic.

It's like a standoff between the frowning faces of the boss and the employee. Both are thinking bad things about the other. I'd like to give you a perspective from a boss's point of view. My hope is that by sharing this other perspective and applying that to your situation, you can check to see if any of this might suggest some behavior changes. I acknowledge that there are bad bosses. I also acknowledge that without reason, some simply don't like you and want you to be gone. Despite this, there are things some employees do that make even the best bosses seem like tyrants.

There are two categories of issues that make employee's situations bad or, at minimum, don't earn any points. These things are absolutely in the control of anyone.

1. Poor performance
2. Bare minimum of work

## Poor Performance

If you aren't performing to the expectations of management, then they say something about this to you. It's hard to feel warm and fuzzy about someone who just said what you did was a flop. It's also easy to think that person is being unreasonable or difficult—yet are they really?

More than anything else, a manager just wants things to work right. They don't dream of coming in to the office and giving someone a bad time about their work. There is a higher amount of energy and focus drain that happens when an employee isn't working up to expectations, because the manager has to go through extra steps to monitor the work. While it is part of management's job, usually the manager's job is not structured in such a way that they really have time for the extra work entailed with overseeing a poorly performing employee. That type of employee creates extra work AND extra stress.

That is only one part of the fun and games for a manger. Add to that the step of sitting down with the employee to tell them the bad news. These are tension-filled confrontations at best and, at worst, a tirade by the employee ensues. This isn't how most managers want to spend their day.

The employee with performance problems almost never really "gets it." If they did, they probably wouldn't have issues to start with. Most managers give the under-performing employee the benefit of the doubt when they start engaging in tough performance-related conversations. (I do acknowledge that there are managers who are such pansies about having a performance conversation that they will wait until they are mad. The conversation is then pretty ugly.) The benefit of the doubt in this case is that if the issue is pointed out, it will be corrected. I have seen instances where, following these chats, the performance actually gets worse and there is often some strange behavior that coincides with the pursuant behavior.

I once had an employee who, in an attempt to portray deep listening, would bulge her eyes and go unblinking for the duration of our performance talks. I thought this had to take so much concentration that she couldn't be listening. She *wasn't* listening and, ultimately, I had to terminate her. It was very unfortunate because I felt she was more than capable of performing.

While performance feedback should be in the form of ongoing and non-threatening dialogues, many times these evaluations simply don't take place. Evaluations are part of your ongoing career development. You are responsible for your job performance, which means you need to ask how you are performing if a manager isn't forthcoming with information about your performance. You want to be proactive by first ensuring you know what the expectations are of your performance. You then need to obtain ongoing input on how you are performing to those expectations. This will allow you the best opportunity to be successful and to avoid poor performance.

My main point is to help you understand that all leaders are responsible for ensuring specific things get done  with the people doing the work. Part of the job includes assessing each employee's performance. This process is not fun for either of you, but later I will give you some steps you can take to ensure poor performance isn't part of what has created your Bad Boss.

### Bare Minimum

I don't know what else to call this section of information about the second thing employees do to worsen their situation with the boss.

What I am talking about is when an employee only does enough to "get by." The work may not be poor enough to warrant a performance conversation, but it also isn't that great. The other part of this is the complete lack of initiative on the part of the employee. You'd be shocked at how frequently this type of employee exists.

A lack of initiative manifests itself in countless ways. It usually means an employee won't do one thing more than what they've been assigned. They wait to be told what to do. A lack of initiative means a manager has to continuously look for business problems the employee needs to solve or improve, when it would be easier for the employee to spot and solve these on their own. No one wins when this situation exists. The manager looks like they are micro-managing because the employee isn't being helpful within the framework of their assigned work. The manager has to operate at a lower level than they'd prefer, leaving other value-add work completely ignored. Work has to be prioritized and the lower level work will always take priority because this work affects basic business functions.

I can tell you from first-hand experience that when a boss has an employee like this, it's a huge disappointment.

Even though people usually don't see things like initiative as part of performance expectations, you can count on this being required. The boss does expect you to "just do it" without being told. If your boss is already prone to emotional reactions and poor social skills, their ability to be somewhat reasonable disappears in this type of situation.

I once told an employee "You want to do everything you can to keep me out of your sandbox, because at any point that I don't think you're doing your job, I will jump in feet first. When I do, I will make it so unpleasant you will do anything to get me out."  I share this story to point out that even kind and gentle people like me will be a nasty hag if your behavior on the job isn't what it needs to be.

# THINGS YOU CAN
# AND SHOULD DO
# TO MANAGE YOUR PERFORMANCE

WE HAVE NOW COVERED a lot of ground to ensure you aren't doing things that may inadvertently create a Bad Boss or make a Bad Boss worse. The final thing to cover is your performance.

If you work for a business that has ongoing performance assessments, you're lucky! From my experience, about fifty-percent of employees have never worked for a place that makes performance management a routine activity. Regardless of this, managing your performance is your responsibility. It's your career and your life, which means you don't want this important function to happen haphazardly. If you do, you risk big ugly surprises that are easy to avoid. For a boss who is not acquainted with the practice of performance evaluations, this may surprise or embarrass them because of their lack of knowledge. You want to introduce them to the reason why you are asking for a review without casting any judgment on them in the process. By managing your performance on an ongoing basis, it makes the discussions easier for both you and your boss. While it can support asking for a raise, the process shouldn't be used only for that purpose. Your performance, and the diligence of managing that performance, should take place more than once a year.

If you handle this process well, your boss may be so impressed they may want to continue using an evaluation process. If you have a Bad Boss, they may be resistant. If that is the case, don't be derailed by their behavior. You can still help yourself tremendously by pursuing each step outlined.

### How to Avoid a Performance Issue: Start with a Baseline

Make sure you understand your responsibilities, tasks, deadlines and any other expectations. While a good manager should cover all these things with you, a Bad Boss may not. You need to take responsibility yourself. You'll also want to occasionally refresh your understanding of these items.

## Document Your Baseline and Update It

Document your responsibilities and the expectations of your output. Make sure you understand both the qualitative and quantitative elements of how you will be measured. When things change, and they will, update your understanding as well as your documentation.

Any documentation you produce should be shared and verified with your boss. This way, it ensures you are on the same page and effective two-way communication has occurred. Even if you can't get them to validate your documentation, you are still operating with their documented input about expectations.

# SEEK PERFORMANCE FEEDBACK
# ON AN ONGOING BASIS

I T'S HARD TO GO astray when you constantly know how you're doing. Seeking the boss's feedback allows you to course-correct before getting too far off track. It also confirms your performance in the mind of the boss, because they are reinforcing good outcomes.

Don't fail to recognize the opinions of others. You should want and expect the input and opinions of others you work with to be part of your performance assessment. While the final opinion of your performance rests with your boss, most of the time the boss is detached from the ongoing, daily work you do. These are people you may work closer with on certain parts of your job. Obtaining their input on your performance provides a better picture of how you are doing. Additionally, your boss may seek out the opinions of other managers or leaders to obtain perspective on your performance. Your work more than likely impacts more than your immediate group or business. You need to know who these "stakeholders" are and ask them for feedback. I have seen bosses think an employee was doing well until someone came to them and filled them in on how crappy their employee was doing. Those opinions matter.

## Document Your Results

We don't always think to document, but it is an important part of solidifying your understanding with those around you. If you work in an environment that requires some kind of status report, this is a perfect opportunity to document what you have done and how the work was done. If you can, include data results that will enhance what you've recorded. If you don't work in that type of situation, produce a monthly recap for your records and copy your boss on the document.

## Proactively Work Issues

If you foresee a problem due to lack of resources, support, priority conflicts, or training, you need to flag those issues for the boss at the first sign of a problem. You need to come to an agreement on how the issue will be resolved. They need to be part of the solution.

## When It Has Gone Bad

If you have done the steps I've outlined, and your boss is still dissatisfied with your performance, all is not lost. You still have the potential to improve your performance and their opinion of your work.

I have seen too many employees ignore the input the boss gives them, even when they were telling the employee they were failing. I've also seen employees give up or start doing things that did not help their situation.

## Listen and Ask Questions

It is hard to avoid being defensive when you are told your performance is lacking, but it will only make matters worse for you if you're combative. When you are trying to defend what you've done, you aren't listening. When you've been told you have missed the mark, you need to understand the difference between what is expected and what you delivered. You need to seek information that will lead you to put together an improvement plan. From my experience, most people simply have a tough time seeing their own behavior versus their intent.

## Develop an Improvement Plan

Document your understanding of where you need to improve, what is expected, and what you're going to do to demonstrate improvement. You should have dates outlined where you will reconvene to review your progress. You don't want the intervals between reviews to be too far apart, because if you are still off course, you need to know quickly. There is no specific timing to recommend. It needs to make sense to the dynamics of the work you perform.

## Don't Over-Compensate

When you are having a hard time delivering the basics, you need to stick with really learning how to do them well. I have seen people in performance trouble decide to start doing things out of their scope of responsibilities or take one element of what they are doing wrong and over-correct. The best analogy I can give you is if you were told you drove too close to the center line and you over-corrected to the point you drove on the shoulder of the road. Over-correction can also be a problem.

Keep in mind that when you are in a performance crisis, this is not the time to be trying to add something new or sexy to your workload. I once had an employee who wasn't performing the basics decide the company should pay for programming classes they wanted to take (which weren't part of their job). While I believe in ongoing improvement, this was not the time to be away from the desk and adding to an already bad situation. Use your head—don't grab an anchor if you're drowning. Needless to say, I wasn't impressed with the lack of judgment and focus by this person.

## Evaluate Yourself

You may not have considered this, but you might be in the wrong job. You may not be suited to the kind of work you've been hired to do. This isn't failure, it's awareness. Because we don't have many tools to help determine the right career, we often end up in careers by default. That default may not support who you authentically are.

You need to evaluate not only your ability to respond to performance expectations, but whether you can sustain and grow from them. A career that is misaligned will cause you years of stress and unhappiness.

## Limit Your Venting

When things aren't going well, we need to release some of the emotion and frustration. Find a neutral person who will let you flap your arms and say nasty things without judging you or participating. You will find, however, that venting and talking over your situation too much will not improve your attitude, but will only make you feel worse, especially if you're doing this with people at work. You want to limit how much venting you do.

There are those people who love a good dust-up. They will gravitate to you like flies to honey and do everything they can to set you off into another emotional frenzy. You need to keep your complaining to a limited set of people, with limited frequency.

Be aware of the problem of venting to a co-worker. While they can relate to the problem you are experiencing, you have to assume most of what you say could get back to the boss. I usually heard what was being said about my actions and decisions, both good and bad, from my employees. I often knew that the people saying those things would have been shocked at how fast those things made their way directly to me. I rarely let on like I was aware of what was being said, but trust me, your venting will get back to the boss. You may think you have a "code of silence" with a good friend/co-worker. It's been my experience (and the experience of other leaders) that some part of what you  say will make its way to the boss. You can't predict how a Bad Boss will react or treat the gossip when it reaches them.

# BAD BOSS STORY #2

## AS TOLD BY A FORMER HR EXECUTIVE
## IN AN HIGH TECH/FORTUNE 500 COMPANY

EARLY IN MY CAREER, I worked for a manufacturing manager to recruit and hire people for his organization. At the same time, my direct manager was in HR in an arrangement known as a matrix report. I was given a quota to hire a specific number of factory workers per week. If that number was missed, even for issues outside my control, the manufacturing manager would inform me that my poor performance was shutting down the factory. I was in constant fear of being fired, at the worst and, at the least, publicly humiliated.

Yelling at his staff and at me was a routine occurrence. More than one time he brought me to tears, although

I didn't cry in front of him. I did everything I could to meet the weekly hiring quota, working inordinately long days and weekends. I would get calls in the middle of the night from him or a member of his staff saying someone was at the front desk with a resume and I should come in to interview the person.

Thankfully, my direct HR manager counseled me to ignore the late-night calls. It was comforting to know my direct manager had my back and wouldn't allow me to be fired for not responding to unreasonable demands.

Feeling more empowerment, I did ignore a late-night call, but I knew the next day I would get raked over the coals in the staff meeting.

When I arrived at the staff meeting the next day, I sat a bag of nails down on the table. When my manager asked what I had brought in the bag, I told him, "I knew you would be crucifying me today, so I decided to bring my own nails." I didn't know if he would kick me out or what he would do. To my surprise, he laughed and said: "Finally, you found your voice!" It was obvious he now respected me for standing up for myself.

From that point forward, we got along just fine. He didn't like or respect people he could push around, which up to that defining moment, I had been. He still criticized and pushed me, but I could now negotiate how I would respond to his outrageous demands.

## My thoughts on this Bad Boss:

It is not uncommon for people (even management) to abuse people they think are weak. Some people do it to test to see how far they will be allowed to go. Others aren't as consciously aware of the dynamic that drives their abuse.

Many people would not have had the courage to eventually stand their ground like this woman did in the same circumstance. She became more empowered when she understood the ultimate decision to fire her was not in the hands of this Bad Boss—and had the assurance that she was protected. I believe she would have ultimately found her own limit, but it would have taken more time.

It is never good to allow anyone to abuse you in or out of a work setting. Granted, there are usually high stakes in these situations that the recipient of the abuse is trying to avoid, thus allowing the abuse to occur. However, we show people how they can treat us and when abuse is left to continue, the situation never improves. Respect is a reciprocal value in relationships and when it is missing, creates a dysfunctional situation.

# MANAGING "UP"

Y OU ARE NOW GOING to learn to Manage Up, as it is the basis of *Accelerating Your Career*. I will outline a number of Bad Boss types later and when I do, you will notice several of the actions I suggest are drawn directly from the "Managing Up" process. I will go a few steps further to customize Managing Up when the dynamics of specific Bad Boss behavior exist. You can think of managing a Bad Boss as the masters' level of Managing Up.

To begin your introduction into Managing Up, it is important for us to be on the same page with the definition.

I define Managing Up as: working for mutual benefit of you and your boss. It is the process of teaching your boss how to manage you and at the same time effectively managing your relationship with your boss. Put another way, it's about establishing a good working relationship with your boss or at least the best one possible.

It is extraordinary to me that people think they can simply go to work and never create relationships. These types tend to think they aren't being paid to socialize. They don't want work and personal to mix and believe if they focus on their work, everything should work well. I can tell you unconditionally that won't be the case.

Like it or not, you have a relationship with everyone you encounter on the job. There is no job on the face of the earth where you can avoid contact with another person and, therefore, a relationship. You may have relationships based on infrequent contact, or a poor relationship, but you still have interaction. The question is whether or not the relationship and interactions are mutually beneficial.

Relationships are based on something in your environment that is connecting you to others. At work, you are connected to others in a big way. Most of the time our work is interdependent on others and the work they do. Most businesses function like the internal cogs of a watch. Each person does something different, but their efforts mesh together for the whole thing to work. When you choose to avoid or ignore the realities of relationships at work, you are choosing a path of great difficulty and eventual failure. Most of the people I have met with this perspective were unhappy, pessimistic, and have a distorted view of how the world works.

I included this little lecture for those people who might decide to blow this off as unimportant. In fact, your relationships will be the single biggest factor for your eventual success, or failure, professionally.

So, you have a choice when it comes to your boss. You can establish a good working relationship, or at least the best one you can have, or put your career in peril.

Assuming you want to develop the best possible working relationship, let's review the various elements of Managing Up.

## Learn What Is Important to the Boss

You could easily think overseeing your job or making sure you earn money for the company is the priority of your boss. While those things are important, you will soon discover that for each person in the same role, there will be different focuses. Each of us have different life views and we approach our jobs, even if they are identical, in different ways.

By learning what is important to your boss, you put yourself in a position to support their goals. How you support those may be bound by your assigned responsibilities, but usually the boundaries are a bit elastic. There will be various parts of your job that will nicely intersect with what the boss prefers. It is the intersection of your job and the boss's priorities where you will want to put your time and attention.

If you are unclear about what is important to your boss, there are several things you can do figure that out. Consider doing any of the following:

**ASK THEM.** You do need to ensure you ask the question in a way that you can get the most meaningful response. Don't ask "yes" or "no" questions. Also, they may initially give you a superficial answer because people are so accustomed to doing that when uncomfortable. A superficial response is not something you should pursue. Also, they could respond with the company "party line" and it still may not be what is hot for them. You'll know when the response is good—they will have energy around what they tell you.

**WHAT THEY FOCUS ON.** We all tend to focus on things we like and are drawn to. We talk about those things, we tinker with them even when we don't have to and may relate other things to them. Everyone does this as well as your manager. All you have to do is pay attention. I know a manager who is an introvert like me and who is also very analytical. The focus of his universe is looking at facts and figures to inform his decisions. I personally think this is a good trait, but not one a lot of people are drawn to. An astute employee of his would do well if they wanted him to support a proposal by arguing the case with data.

**WHAT THEY REWARD.** This could be trickier, but even if

the boss isn't handing out awards, they may be praising or promoting people who deliver according to their priorities.

**WHAT'S IMPORTANT TO THE BOSS'S BOSS?** Even if it is the customer, we all serve someone, and that includes your boss. Many times, your boss will be doing the same thing you are, which means if you can help them look good to the people who matter, you've done well.

Of course, simply understanding what is important to the boss is not enough if you don't do anything with it. Your task is to identify how you can support these priorities and, in the process, communicate along the way. You will gain the boss as a supporter.

The only word of caution is to ensure you aren't trading off a critical deliverable that is part of your core responsibility for a high-priority item for the boss. If you are facing this type of situation, you should first check with your boss for agreement to change expectations. I've seen this backfire where an employee eagerly pursued something that looked great to the boss only for the boss to later discover a ball was dropped in the process. This then calls into question your judgment, communication and, quite frankly, your integrity. You will lose any ground you may have gained if you don't handle your work priorities openly.

Your goal is to become indispensable, and the best way to do that is to know the priorities of your boss and deliver results while at the same time keeping your own work priorities in mind.

## Yes, You Have to Take Responsibility to Change

I will point out the obvious theme in this book. You have to change what and how you interact with others and certainly each boss you will have. I have had countless people get on their high-horse thinking they shouldn't have to do anything different. The attitude is "take me as I am  and if you can't get along with me, you have a problem." That attitude is immature and egotistical. It's also one that will never allow for success in life and work. The world does not center on your way of doing things. You only have control over the things you do—and in the case of working well with others, you have to be the one responsible for accommodating another person.

The same high-minded people will also make an argument that when you change your behavior around different people you are being disingenuous or dishonest. As they see it, changing behavior violates core values. Your behavior *does change* to suit the situation and it always has. You learn as an infant that you will be more successful with Mom when you do certain things and with Dad those things will be different. That insight broadens throughout your life unless you choose to be inflexible and difficult at some point.

What I am pointing out in this book are the various things for you to consider, observe, and act on, that will lead to your success.

## How They Operate

We all have different operating modes. By that, I'm saying there are things like how we communicate, how we learn, right down to how we organize our work. These modes of operating are driven largely by habit and personality. Just like you, every boss is different, and you want to learn how your boss operates so you can respond to what works most effectively for them.

One way you can discover how your boss operates is if your group, including the boss, has taken personality assessments. Usually, when this is done as a group, the outcome of the assessments is shared in order to help everyone work together more productively. If this has occurred, you want to pay close attention to how you operate compared to your boss. You may discover you have opposing operating modes.

You can also ask your boss if they have taken any personality assessments that they would be willing to share to aid you in working together more effectively.

Additionally, consider the following:

## Personality Differences

In the past decade, more and more personality assessments are emerging. There is finally more acknowledgement that many business problems are created by virtue of the people doing the work lacking the skills to work together effectively.

You may have a Bad Boss because you have personality differences. If that is even some of what might be at play, you're in luck! There are many books and assessments to help you further understand various aspects to both your personality and the personalities of others.

Simply understanding personality types isn't enough if you don't identify where the potential for conflict exists and figure out how to adjust accordingly. The point of all this information about personalities is to help you understand other people better and to help you interact with them effectively. Unfortunately, I've seen too many people and organizations take personality assessments only to return to work with no plans to do anything differently.

If the group you work in has taken personality assessments, pull them out now and start analyzing you and your boss. If you haven't done anything like this, I suggest taking the Meyers-Briggs' test. There are also many books and sites on the Internet that will educate you. By learning more about personality differences, you can adapt to fit the situation with the boss. Oftentimes, our conflict with another person stems from personality differences and an inability to understand how we might modify our approach. A good skill to have is observing personality preferences and accommodating those differences in order to maximize your ability to establish a good working relationship.

Even if you make improvements to accommodate the personality of your Bad Boss, doing so is not a magic pill. I learnt while I was getting my Meyers-Briggs instructor certification that with a problematic person, you might still have a disorder going on that adds another personality layer over that "type." Adjusting to personality types like those won't help—then of course, the Bad Boss may just be a jerk.

I believe when it comes to adjusting your behavior to accommodate personality differences, these are the areas you may look to change:

- Communication style
- Learning style
- Planning style
- Relating or social style

## Communication Style

Since communication style is a huge component to all successful interactions, I'd like to offer up some ideas about things to look for and actions to take.

## Too Little Information

This issue is the most common. We often skip over key pieces of information and make assumptions about what the other person does or does not know (if we even give any topic that much thought). Some people feel reluctant to ask questions or pursue the boss for more information. If that's you, you aren't helping your situation. Ask questions and go after the information you need, because you are the only one who will have to live with the consequences.

## Too Much Information

Some people offer up too much, too detailed, and too technical information, which for some people will turn them off. If this is your tendency and your boss prefers to gloss-over details, they may go so far as to avoid you or be rude to you simply to shut you up. You might think all the detail is important. It may be to you, but at the next level up, it isn't. Summarize and ask if they want more detail. If they do, they'll let you know.

On the other hand, if your boss is the one who goes into copious detail, it can result in the following possible issues:

- The directions are confusing

- You may feel insulted with the implication that they have to tell you how to do your job

- If you aren't good with too much detail, you may stop listening or adopt body language of contempt or disinterest. That will not earn you points.

- If this is your situation, you should consider asking for their input in an alternate method, for example, if the boss is speaking, ask them to send you an email.

- If the boss resists your request for communicating in another method, consider taking notes and putting them in an email. Then send them to the boss and request their

agreement that you are on the right path.
Taking notes and documenting will help you
to listen and clarify information.

## Frequency

There is no rule of thumb that says you should communicate daily or at any interval of time. The best way to think about frequency is to think first about events or milestones.

If you have a deliverable, communicate to the boss and key players what to expect and when. Depending on how long it takes to get a result or a milestone along the way, you can use the milestones as the timing to provide updates. When you accomplish a result, that is also the time to communicate.

If you are working on something that is going to take an extended period of time to accomplish, then find out from the boss and key players how frequently they would like to hear from you.

Another critical time to communicate is any time there is a change in direction or outcome. Nasty surprises are never good, even with the best boss.

## Learning Style

We all take in information and learn in a mix of different ways. Just like personality types, none of us are only one way in all situations. Generally, most people have a couple of dominant ways to learn.

I'm outlining learning styles because in a work setting

we are in a constant state of learning and taking in information from each other. You could easily categorize this as communications, but I address learning styles separately because this simplifies things considerably and makes this easier to learn and implement.

To remain simple (as there are entire books and classes on learning styles), there are three primary ways people take in or learn information:

1. **VISUAL** – People learn by what they see either in pictures, videos, through reading, through presentations, or by observation. I have also noticed that within this category there is a subset preference.

   I worked for an executive who was on top of his game if you gave him information to read before you had a meeting to discuss the subject. In that regard, he was a classic introvert. He had to have time to absorb and process information before reaching any decision. His learning style was through reading. In a meeting focused on discussion, he couldn't read something for the first time and be able to fully participate.

2. **AUDITORY** – People learn by what they hear from lectures, recordings or discussions. They can read something, but not fully grasp the information without the auditory component to help them comprehend. You will notice in many classroom settings that material is read out loud. This is

done to appeal to the auditory learners in a group.

In the example I gave previously, reading helped the executive to participate in discussions and to make faster decisions. If he wasn't given a chance to do that, he focused more on reading during the meetings instead of participating in the discussion. In the same meeting, there were other executives who would have blown off any reading material before the discussion. If you don't understand these differences, you might be frustrated by attempts to share materials with your boss that get ignored.

3. **TACTILE/KINESTHETIC** – Some people learn by doing, moving or touching. You can think about this as a demonstration of something with an interactive component to it.

   I once worked with a peer-manager who often stood or even paced during meetings. At the time, I thought it was nervous energy, but it seems there are people who learn better if their body is in motion. He also preferred to discuss things while walking.

Discover which learning style your boss has and engage with them in that manner.

## Planning Style

Planning is one of those things you either love or hate. Most people in a business setting realize you can rarely get anything done without some amount of planning. The people who fall into the category of hating to plan sometimes figure out ways to adapt to those demands but may do the minimal amount to get by.

While you are observing your boss and thinking about personality, pay attention to their planning style versus your own. When there are two polar opposites they tend to have fairly strong reactions and beliefs about each other.

**PLANNER** – In the extreme, a person who loves to plan will want everything planned, including free time. Their belief about a person who doesn't plan is that they "fly by the seat of their pants." They think of non-planners as disorganized and in need of overseeing in order to get work done.

**NON-PLANNER** – Probably not the best label, but this person takes in information and allows for a certain amount of spontaneous, timely events to inform the final outcome. You can't see their planning, as it can often be done in their head . . . and just in time to execute the work. Their belief about planners is that they are stiff, inflexible, and lack a certain amount of creativity.

If you and your Bad Boss have opposite planning styles, you will need to accommodate the differences to ensure you minimize the negative effects.

## Relating or Social Styles

As a human, we do require some amount of interaction and contact with others, but the degree of relating varies widely. Like many of the things I've mentioned, when you have opposites together, those differences can easily become a source of problems unless adjustments are made.

It's important to remember that just like most people who react negatively when they encounter a person who is "difficult" to interact with, the boss is no different. If the Bad Boss finds your social style irritating, they may have removed the filter for containing their irritation. To understand some of the considerations for social styles, consider looking for these traits:

## High Relationship Need

People who have high relating-needs require a level of relationship with another person in order for them to be able to comfortably work together. You will see them first interact with others through greetings, asking somewhat superficial questions, and they may even kick into a bit of non-business conversation. People who don't respond in equal measure to someone with high-relating needs can either have fluid interactions shut down entirely, or the person with high-relating needs may have difficulty fully engaging with them or act put off by them.

When the priority of relating hasn't been met for this type of person, they often view the non-relating person as rude, hard-driving, and unfriendly. Of course, that could be untrue, but a high-relating need person doesn't like a person who doesn't take the time to treat them "right."

## Low Relationship Need

People who have low-relating need require little or no relationship in order to work with someone else. You will see this person by-pass greetings and small talk and immediately begin to discuss the topic of their focus. When this person encounters greetings and small talk, they may find it distracting and unnecessary. When the low-relating person is unable to return to the focus of their topic quickly, they can become easily frustrated because they are becoming impatient.

A low-relating need person will often view a high-relating person as doing too much unnecessary, unfocused talking and as wasting time. They want to get to the point and move on.

One of the ways I think about the difference in these two styles is, what is of highest priority in his or her interactions? With the first style the priority is relating first and covering business topics second. With the second style the priority is business topics first and relating second. As you can see (and can probably relate to), you can really get on the last nerve of someone like a Bad Boss if you are out of step with their social style.

## Ask

You are going through a process to learn what will work best with your boss. I'm always surprised at how little people actually communicate in work and personal life. Asking questions is the root of learning and communicating. The simplest way to learn the preferred operating mode for your boss is to ask them.

Use the categories I've listed above (communication, planning, etc.) and ask your boss what works best for them and enhance what you are told by the information you observe. Most people do know what works and what annoys them, so finding out is all part of you learning how to work well the boss.

## Teach Them Your Job

Never make the assumption that your boss knows your job. They may have a conceptual understanding of it enough to ask you fairly intelligent questions, but that may be where their knowledge ends.

When you newly acquire a boss, either through a new job or reorganization, that is the best time to begin the process of educating the boss about your job. In that process, you should also outline what the expectations of you in that job have been and gain agreement of those standards. They may elect to change those standards later, but you have at least established a baseline.

Even if you are beginning to Manage Up with a boss you've had for a while, you are not setting up a formal training time. Rather, you are simply being deliberate in your communication to share a bit more detail about what, why, and how you are doing your work. You want to be careful to avoid technical terminology or be too detailed.

You are trying to accomplish several things with your boss. First, if they have a good grasp of your work, they may gain a greater appreciation for what you do and the impact you have. Second, they can be more creative, not only in assigning you work, but in developing solutions to business problems. Third, when they assign you work they are in a better position to counsel with you on priority tradeoffs, if needed. One of the things that can make an okay boss seem like a Bad Boss is when they assign work when they are completely clueless that they have created an unworkable situation for you. You can avoid that situation if the boss has a good understanding of your work.

## Take Initiative

Who doesn't love a person who will jump in and make things happen? It's a highly desirable trait and one that is less prevalent than you might realize. It's also what every boss would love to see out of his or her employees. As you might guess, they are often disappointed. A disappointed boss is not a happy boss. Keep that in mind.

Initiative is a trait that describes leaders. You can't have a leader if this trait is missing, even if all other positive traits are present. This attribute is the key to promotions and greater responsibility. (Does it sound like I'm a big fan of initiative?)

Needless to say, if you demonstrate initiative you will win points and be a standout among your work peers. It's also a vital facet of Managing Up.

What do you need to do to demonstrate initiative? Nothing difficult. If the following actions aren't ones you do routinely, you have new habits to form.

## Do More Than Expected

It is still critical that you perform to the expectations you were given to do your job. In doing those things, take one extra unexpected step to do something that will add value to the business—then make that extra step noticeable to your boss.

## Take Ownership

Think like you own the business. Business owners naturally are looking at the bottom line and what needs to happen to improve the business. When you start thinking as if you co-owned the business, you look at the work differently. You automatically give yourself permission to be creative or go the extra step.

## Generate Ideas

Don't expect the boss to have all the ideas for new innovations or ways to solve problems. No one has all the answers, including the boss. Take the perspective that you are contributing to a list of possible options to be pursued. Not all of them will be acted on and that doesn't matter. What does matter is that your boss recognizes that you are thinking about improvements and you're creative. When they need some ideas, they'll know you are the "go-to" person.

## Be Assertive and Speak Up

Asserting your opinions, ideas, and actions is an important element of initiative. No boss wants to have to drag information or action out of an employee. Be forthcoming and confident in asserting yourself once you have thought through what needs to be said or done.

One of the problems we often have is becoming too sensitive about our ideas and actions once we have given them life. Sometimes when we feel questioned or disagreed with, we retreat and vow to not take initiative again. Feeling that way is understandable but staying hidden isn't going to help you Manage Up or be successful. Learn and move on with assertive behaviors.

I had a client who had done some self-assessment about his past behavior with a former boss. He had not been forthcoming with updates to the boss, nor had he provided the boss with any reports. He had waited passively for the boss to ask. When the boss finally asked, he gave the boss 40+ page documents, which only angered his boss. He had not taken the initiative to find out what the boss wanted and what would be the most effective way to provide him with the reports. He essentially forced the boss into demanding information, then gave him too much information to use effectively. My client understands better what he should have done and will never repeat that mistake in the future. This is a good example of how assertiveness plays a role in managing the relationship.

## Solve Problems

If you think about it, a huge part of all jobs is to solve problems. If everything worked perfectly, we would never have jobs. In taking initiative, you are looking to solve problems you have not been asked to solve. There are always more problems to solve in a business that there are  resources to solve them, so you never have to worry about running out of opportunities. You will be a valuable resource to the boss and your co-workers if you routinely find issues and solve them.

## Think Ahead

It's easy to take a short view of the road in front of us. Daily problems crop up and become priorities. Urgency results in us taking our eyes off the future. (Even if the future is a month from now.) You can be the voice that periodically asks, "what should we be thinking about next?" If the boss knows you are thinking beyond today, that helps them think the same way and it gives them confidence that fewer things will sneak up to bite them.

## Volunteer

You can ask to be given assignments or projects that the boss discusses. It makes you more noticeable and gives you a chance to learn new things of value.

## Communicate Frequently

Communication is notoriously the weak spot in all relationships and organizations. It's a huge plus for your career if you train your boss to expect to hear from you on all critical matters on a timely basis AND in a way that works for them.

## Make It Easy to Work with You

You'd be surprised to learn that employees are often their own worst enemy. The range of possibilities for what might be an impediment is too numerous to outline. It could cover everything from personality quirks, communication style or lack of communication, all the way to responsiveness to emails or phone calls.

The best analogy is to think about a business you would drive to. If there is road construction that won't allow you to access a business in the normal way, the difficulty may be too great for you and you'll drive away. The same is true of a working relationship.

I once had a man working for me who hated authority. He made that point to me the first time we met. He didn't want me to be telling him how to do his job, didn't want me to make demands on him, and didn't want to be accountable for keeping me updated on what he was doing. Basically, he wanted to be left alone to do his job. I could see he wasn't going to make working with him easy. In fact, he was going to be a pain. I told him I was fine with his independence, but if he failed to communicate with me, I would become the poster child for the authority he hated most. Also, as his boss, he needed to come to expect that I would give him direction and that constituted his condition for remaining employed. He did not attempt to Manage Up, which was unfortunate, and he remained difficult to work with. Needless to say, he was never given promotions or new opportunities. His loss. My pain.

Your job is to think through whether or not you have made working with you easy or difficult. If you don't know, ask a few people for feedback.

## Deliberately Develop a Relationship

I deliberately left this one for last. I believe if you have done the things I have outlined so far, you will have done a lot to develop a productive relationship. Notice I have not said a friendship, as that is not what you are pursuing. The distinction is primarily one of feeling affection for your boss and that is not necessary. What *is* necessary is that you have developed mutual respect and are connected in such a way that you can both feel a sense of reciprocity.

In my book *Easier Networking*, I outline the four building blocks to developing a relationship. These building blocks apply to ALL relationships no matter if they are personal or professional, with the boss, or a perspective partner. You will see how these building blocks are interwoven into the actions necessary to Manage Up.

## BLOCK #1:
## COMMONALITY

You have to have something in common with another person to start a relationship. Those conditions may change in the future but have to exist to draw you and another person together. In the case of your boss, you have the business in common and possibly the work group you are both in.

## BLOCK #2:
## INFORMATION EXCHANGE AND MUTUAL SUPPORT

Every person you know is an information resource for you. Information is needed to function at work and outside of work. If you are communicating as I have outlined, you are exchanging information.

You will also notice the first thing I listed in Managing Up was to find out what is important to your boss and then deliver to meet those requirements. That is support. The boss is supporting you through ongoing guidance, coaching and training.

## BLOCK #3:
## SHARED VALUES AND CHEMISTRY

As you spend more time getting to know a person, you begin to understand their values. If their values intersect with yours, the relationship deepens. The other thing you can't overlook is chemistry or, put another way, do you like this person? And do they like you? When you like a person, it creates a magnetic pull for the relationship.

## BLOCK #4:
## INVESTMENT OF TIME

Relationships are not developed instantly. They take time and effort, which is the only real currency we all have. You must invest your time, which you are doing by the various things you are doing in Managing Up. Over time, this effort will yield you a productive relationship with your boss.

I hope you see that with everyone in your life, other than family, you had to develop a relationship by using these four relationship building blocks. With your boss, you need to be mindful and deliberate about developing and managing the relationship.

# BAD BOSS STORY #3

### KRISTEN CLARK:
#### CONFIDENCE COACH, AWARD-WINNING AUTHOR,
#### EDITOR, PUBLISHER
www.AmericanMuttPress.com

I WORKED FOR A MAN who is best described as a busybody. He lacked any personal boundaries and frequently stuck his nose where it didn't belong. His behavior was often unacceptable but tolerated because of his brilliance.

At the office, he had a way of nosing into things by assigning the task of participating in projects owned by other groups and departments just so he could learn what was going on. I was often asked to participate in something that neither my department, nor I, had any role or stake in.

Thankfully, I was able to establish solid working relationships with the people and leaders in other groups in order to gather information my boss wanted. It helped me to be open and direct, although one time I had a department manager rake me over the coals for inquiring about things I had no business knowing. Her sting was harsh, but gave me great insight about what my boss was charging me off to do. I quickly learned what was within the scope of my job and department so I could discern for myself whether or not his assignments were appropriate to pursue. Once I had figured this out, I decided to push back on some of his assignments. I wasn't always successful, though, as he didn't necessarily recognize any limits on where our participation made sense or not. But those were battles I chose carefully.

**My thoughts on this Bad Boss:**

This is a good example of several things:

A company will often allow management to continue to do things that aren't appropriate or productive simply because they pander to the expertise. I never think you should be held hostage by someone's talents, but you see this occur fairly often.

This illustrates the importance of good work relationships. Kristen was able to supply the Bad Boss with more information than she might have gathered had she not worked on developing these relationships. She never compromised her values, as she was always very open about what she was trying to accomplish. Good communication often wins the day, even when what you are doing isn't well supported.

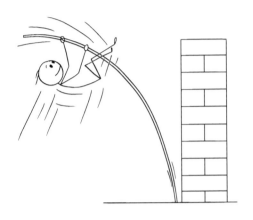

# MANAGING YOUR BAD BOSS

## YOUR BAD BOSS IS LIKE DEALING
## WITH DIFFICULT PEOPLE

I N THE GRAND SCHEME of life, we quickly learn we can interact with most people in what I would call "default mode." In other words, we can use the same behavior repeatedly and can be fairly successful in doing so. The rub starts when the standard default doesn't work very well with another person.

Logically, all of us realize we are a diverse species. We know we come in all sizes, colors and backgrounds. Despite that keen knowledge, we aren't necessarily agile in dealing with diverse personalities. When our one-size-fits-all way of interacting with others doesn't go as well as expected, the knee-jerk reaction is to think the other person is somehow bad, or . . . fill in the blank.

We don't automatically think about adjusting or adapting to the style of others, even though that is exactly what our thinking should be. There is only one mental control panel we have access to—our own! We can't control or change someone else—as much as we'd like to sometimes. We do need to change our reactions and mode when our standard doesn't seem to work.

When we're talking about working with a difficult person, you have to understand there is really only one primary thing that isn't meshing: communication. The other person has a communication style that doesn't align well with you and perhaps others. Or it may be *your* communication style. The communication style is made worse when there is little or no "social currency" between you and the difficult person. When we have even a slightly developed relationship with another person, that goes a long way to compensate for poor communication.

Many of the things taught in conflict management can be applied to a situation where a boss or another person requires being approached differently. Let's look at some approaches from conflict management and tweak them slightly for your use. These approaches are useful not only during actual conflict but anytime you're dealing with difficult people.

## Listen at a Deeper Level

We all have the capacity to listen to others at a level deeper than words. Stay present with the person and don't apply your own assumptions or personalize what is being said. When you listen at this deeper level you are able to understand intent and other issues going on with another person. You are better able to observe body language.

## Ask Questions and Paraphrase Your Understanding

It's fascinating how few people will seek first to understand another person. When interacting, especially with a difficult person, you need to ask questions to clarify what they are saying. When you paraphrase back to them in your own words what you do understand that gives both people an opportunity to adjust terminology and go deeper with explanations. All too often, I see people walking away from conversations confused and hostile when they had every opportunity to create a different result. This process can take more time, but the time spent on the front-end of a conversation or relationship is a small investment when compared to negative outcomes.

## Remain Calm and Assume the Motives of the Other Person Are Good

Particularly at work, most people simply want to do a good job and achieve the assignments they are given. If you assume the other person has those things in mind, you will usually feel okay about your interactions, even if the other person lacks a certain amount of social grace.

It's important to note that when confusion or anger enter into your interactions, the conversation will never go well. Those emotions can create defensiveness and shut down listening. It's my observation that when a person becomes defensive, they have selective hearing.

## Don't Personalize the Other Person's Actions

Granted, the boss may be focused on you or your performance, but the worst reaction you can have is to assume the boss or another person is out to get you. In fact, they have probably spent almost no time giving you a second thought and more time thinking about their own concerns. You play a role in an issue or resolution and that's why they are focused on you. Also, when you over- personalize someone else's actions, you have automatically positioned yourself as a victim. You rarely have a positive outcome as a victim.

## Project Warmth

You'd be surprised how much better your interactions will go when you smile and relax. Make eye contact and physically lean in slightly to the other person during interactions. Although these are small gestures, they can be significant body language signals letting others know you are approachable and interested.

## Take the Perspective That Working Effectively with a Challenging Person Is a Puzzle to Solve

When it comes to working with a difficult person or

boss, you now know your standard approach no longer applies. That means you will have to experiment to see what adaptations you can make that will change the situation. Look for clues on how this person prefers to communicate. Generally speaking, poor communication is about not enough information sharing, confusion in communication, or both. You have to look at both you and the other person's style for the solution.

## Avoidance

If you are avoiding interactions with your Bad Boss or difficult person, you are potentially creating a bigger problem. While I do think there are people and situations that call for avoidance, your engagement with a challenging person is really a delicate balancing act. The issue with avoidance means you are most likely missing communications with the Bad Boss and that is never helpful. Avoidance is an understandable reaction to a person you don't like to be around, but it doesn't do anything to build a better relationship or promote communications. The best course of action is to ensure regular communication so you aren't missing any input or missing opportunities where you can provide updates or ask questions.

# TYPES OF BAD BOSSES
## AND WHAT TO DO ABOUT THEM

### The Hovering Helicopter Bad Boss

THIS BAD BOSS IS sometimes known as the "helicopter boss." They seem to have nothing better to do than lurk over your shoulder while you're trying to get your work done. To add insult, they may nit-pick and even rework what you've done. You're left wondering why they hired you in the first place, if they can spend so much time hovering over your job instead of doing their own.

There are a number of potential causes for this:

- They are too controlling. They think they are the only one who can truly get things done right, or they want to see the work done a certain way. They really might not have enough of their own work to do.

- They think hovering is equal to managing and don't really know or understand what they should be doing instead.

- You really might warrant their behavior, because you aren't performing up to standards or you do things that undermine confidence in your work (like you continuously ask to be double-checked.)

You need to understand the reason, or combination of reasons, for their over-involvement in your work. Even if they are killing time just chatting you up, it is still impacting your ability to get your job done in a timely manner. Let's look at some potential actions you can take, once you've identified the cause of their behavior:

**IF THEY'RE CONTROLLING.** Ask for training and performance expectations. Once you've been adequately trained, keep track of your performance and report it to your boss. After enough time of seeing that you are meeting their standards, they will most likely back off. If they are reworking your work, ask for feedback on how to improve so they don't have to take their time redoing your work.

**IF THEY'RE CONTROLLING AND TRAINING AND**

**PERFORMANCE HASN'T CAUSED THEM TO BACK OFF.** Have a discussion. You don't want this to be a defensive conversation, but a problem-solving one. You can open the conversation with something like, "I've noticed you have a strong need to be involved with the work I'm performing. Since I'm meeting the performance expectations, I thought I would find out if there is anything you might need from me that I'm not doing that will make you more comfortable with my work? I just want us to be efficient." Stated this way, you're taking ownership for giving the boss what they need.

**THEY DON'T HAVE ENOUGH WORK OF THEIR OWN.** We've talked about Managing Up. Here's a perfect situation. You can make suggestions or come up with ideas for things that seem appropriate for them to do. If they like the idea, you can always ask, "Do you want to run with this or do you want me to?" Certainly, they might give it to you, but chances are they're looking for something to fill their time. You also need to manage your time. If they are chatting you up due to boredom, return the chat for a short time and then make a brief statement such as, "I need to get back to work." Then turn yourself to the task at hand. Remain friendly.

**IF THEY THINK THIS IS WHAT A MANAGER DOES.** When they approach you, ask if you can help them. Once the request is fulfilled, turn back to your work and ignore them. You will have to get used to their presence and still get your work done.

**IF YOU AREN'T PERFORMING.** Consider this the price you

pay to get back on track. Make sure you understand how to perform the work and what the expectations are. It's not fun having the bad boss in your sandbox, but until you get your performance up to standards, you will see them far more than you desire.

A helicopter boss isn't the worst person in the world to work for, but they are annoying and sometimes ego deflating, especially if they constantly question your work. It can feel like they don't trust you, which may not be the case. Taking the appropriate action can help both of you.

## The Bad Boss Who Can't Communicate

You know this kind of boss. What they say and how they say it leaves you completely befuddled about what they are trying to convey. To add to this, they might be yelling while delivering this completely incomprehensible tirade. Are we having fun yet? Just because they're the boss, doesn't mean they are a pillar of perfect communication. Effective communication is one of the singularly important, yet difficult, business practices to master. When you ascend to the power throne, communication is a critical part of the job. Just because the bad boss has the job, doesn't mean they automatically have mastered the skill of communication.

Communication is a two-way endeavor. There is the giver and the receiver. Both people have a function to perform. The giver has to convey the message in such a way that the receiver has the best possible chance of comprehending what's conveyed. The receiver is not passive. The receiver's role is to ensure their understanding of the message. The best situation is one that can be interactive through questions and validation. Even practicing this, communication just doesn't always work well. Also, it's not just the boss communicating to you, it's you communicating to them. There is nothing worse than a Bad Boss who looks like a deer in the headlights after you speak to them.

The primary career issue with a boss with poor communication skills is that they can impact your performance due to misdirection and misunderstanding. Poor performance leaves a bad impression with those around you and is the opposite of career enhancing. No one really cares if the genesis of your poor performance is due to the boss. You're expected to push through the situation. You have to change your behavior, because you can't expect the boss to.

### What Can You Do to Be More Effective with a Boss Who Is a Poor Communicator?

- **DIFFERENT PEOPLE "TAKE IN" INFORMATION IN DIFFERENT WAYS.** In the past decade much has been said about learning styles. Essentially, what is being taught is that not all people comprehend information/communication the same way. Some people do well in person and through oral communication. Some people do better with things that are written, presented, or with diagrams, and sometimes even through demonstration. If the boss isn't giving or receiving well with the primary mode, switch it. I had a boss who was truly bad in their oral delivery. No amount of questions for clarification changed this. I started asking her to email her direction and thoughts to me, and the communication really improved. She was a good writer and expressed herself better using that mode. She received just fine with oral discussion, she just couldn't give instructions in return. You need to start looking at what part of the communication process is not working, then change it.

- **IF THEY'RE YELLING.** If you are at all like me, you stop listening whenever someone starts yelling. You're overcome with the emotion and impact of that delivery. It's also demoralizing to be yelled at. You should consider a private discussion about the issue of yelling and help them understand the impact on you and your work. You might also learn a few things about the boss that will help mitigate some of those reactions. I once told my boss, right on the spot, "If you really need for me to hear you, you will have to stop yelling." Short and sweet. It worked.

- **VALIDATE YOUR UNDERSTANDING.** I see many people fall short in this area. You need to test if you understand a message by asking questions and paraphrasing back what you think you heard. Many people simply receive a message, get confused, and walk away. That will not help you.

We can all use ongoing improvement in our communications. You might even suggest department training on effective communications or at least read up on the subject. It will enhance your skill set and make you more effective, even when you have a bad boss.

## The Bad Boss Who Takes Credit for Your Work

Among the many things that bad bosses have been known to do is to take credit for your hard work or ideas. You don't like it when a peer does that, but with that group, you feel you might have some recourse to stifle what they're doing. What do you do when a boss takes credit?

The line between a legitimate ethics violation and simply representing innovation in the department can at times be hard to tell. There are some perspectives to consider before taking any action.

You need to understand that the boss has a job to do and that job is not only directing your work and that of your peers, but also "managing up" with their own boss. Their boss is looking for continual improvement in results of the organization, along with the dialogue of what innovative ideas the group is coming up with to stay competitive. In other words, the discussion frequently doesn't involve the specific person who accomplished something or the origin of ideas or proposals. Certainly, that type of information has its usefulness with the big boss for such things as promotions, salary increases, or tactical decisions. The higher you go in the managerial food chain, the less detail is desired. There may be times when your boss is speaking to other people in your organization and refers to your work or ideas without giving you credit. There are several possibilities for why they aren't giving you credit at that time:

- It's not relevant to the discussion.

- Your work or idea may be part of an overall direction the boss has identified and there may be a number of people in the mix.

- Your idea may be a spinoff of something the boss has been talking about or a spinoff of a group discussion.

- They may have legitimately forgotten who the originator was.

In other words, you may be sensitive about getting credit for things when there is no need to be. You need to look at the circumstances of their actions to see if their behavior genuinely warrants your reactions. However, there are times—and certainly bad bosses—who will blatantly represent your work and ideas as their own, and perhaps do the same with your peers, on a consistent basis. It is this situation that calls for some careful footwork. The biggest issue is not so much what they did, it's the possible impact on your career. In order for you to get promotions and growth, the people above you have to observe your accomplishments, growth and potential. It's not always obvious at that level to know the details, so they may rely on your boss to be the one to fill them in. If your boss is using your work to advance their own growth without providing any support for you on the way up, you have a problem to deal with.

What can you do without stepping on a land mine?

Here are some suggestions:

- **PRIVATELY ASK THEM IF THEY REMEMBERED THAT YOU ORIGINATED THE WORK.** Have a non-defensive discussion to let them know what you noticed in an effort to get their version of why the omission took place. Discuss how the gaff can be rectified and move on. Don't attempt to nail them, it will only go bad.

- **DOCUMENT AND PUBLISH YOUR IDEAS AND WORK.** If your organization does status reports, this is a perfect time to put in black and white your great work. It also makes it more difficult for others to stake a claim. Even if your group doesn't openly publish status reports, you can still do one each month and copy your boss, along with any other key players you think would benefit. Look at this as a form of communication.

- **WHEN IT'S TIME FOR THE ANNUAL RAISE/ PERFORMANCE REVIEW, DOCUMENT YOUR ACCOMPLISHMENTS PRIOR TO THE PROCESS BEING KICKED OFF.** This way, it will help the boss remember your results.

- **LOOK FOR PUBLIC OPPORTUNITIES TO SUBTLY INJECT A BIT OF OWNERSHIP INTO YOUR WORK AND IDEAS.** This is known as self-promotion, which makes some people cringe. The deal is, if you don't promote yourself, who will?

When the bad boss takes credit for your work, it's insulting and degrades any environment for trust. Most of the time, these bosses really aren't trying to rob you of any glory, but they're being thoughtless. You can adjust both your thinking and, when needed, your behavior to make sure your career stays on course.

## The Bad Boss Who Is Incompetent

To make sure we're on the same page about an incompetent boss and not just a way to be nasty about your Bad Boss, let's get on the same page.

An incompetent boss is one who isn't functionally adequate or doesn't have sufficient knowledge, skills, judgment or strength. If this is what you're talking about, then you're right—they are incompetent. It happens. In other words, the boss doesn't know squat about being a manager and probably knows little to nothing about the area of work you do.

While it can be frustrating to have an incompetent boss, an incompetent boss can seriously damage or derail your career. If they do have a serious lack of knowledge, they can do nothing to grow you as an employee, which means any growth will be yours to make happen. Let's look at the potential damage they can inflict and what you can do to minimize or avoid that damage.

## Career Impact of an Incompetent Bad Boss:

- **BAD DECISIONS** – Because they don't know your work, the decisions they make can have an impact they are clueless about. They lack insight and understanding. This means the impact to you can range from cleaning up a mess to putting you in a position that makes you look like you tanked the business. It can make you lose precious time and focus . . . or even get fired.

- **BAD DIRECTION** – We look for our boss to provide direction in the form of "how to" all the way to yearly planning. When the boss is incompetent, their directions can be bad or pointless, and often leave important issues untouched.

- **BAD SUPPORT** – Your boss can be the single biggest supporter of your career trajectory, but if they are clueless about the nature of your work, they may be supporting either the wrong things or person. You can't expect them to really know or understand if you're delivering well. They may be a roadblock to your career or simply no help.

When you have an incompetent boss, you have to think through how this person functions in order to use whatever strengths they do have to your advantage—or, at minimum, avoid career-limiting outcomes. Let's look at some of the things you can do to prevail with an incompetent boss:

- **"UP LEVEL" YOURSELF.** In other words, leadership can come from you. If you know your area well, there is no reason to not go ahead to create and pursue direction that you know will achieve results that will be good for your company. Peers follow people who do this naturally, considering them an informal leader. Management—although maybe not your direct boss—will notice your initiative. Of course, you don't want to do something that undermines the boss, so keep them in the loop.

- **FIGURE OUT THE PROBLEM SPOTS.** The boss's incompetence is annoying, but it usually impacts you and others in specific ways, too. Try to observe what those are and make a plan to counteract the problem. I once had an incompetent boss. The biggest issue was that he would sometimes make decisions for the group I managed that were ill-considered and negatively impacted the company. I sat down with him and asked if I could either be involved in those decision discussions or to direct the person to me. This process worked most of the time. There were times when that direction simply wasn't possible, but people soon learned that they needed to come to me for good decisions. We worked around the problem.

- **TEACH THEM.** Every time you speak to your boss you have an opportunity to train and teach them about your area. It seems kind of ludicrous to train your boss, but the ongoing investment will be worth it once they are savvy enough to know what you're talking about.

- **LOOK FOR A MENTOR.** Just because your boss doesn't bring much to the table in the way of helping your growth in the company doesn't mean there isn't someone in your place of business who can be good for your career. Look around for someone at a higher level who is sharp and going places. Hopefully, they have some type of a good connection with you. Ask them to be your mentor. It will be flattering to them and helpful to you to have someone helping you and in your corner.

- **LEAVE.** Sometimes it's better for your career to leave instead of trying to stick it out. If you've tried several things and there is no improvement, it may be time for you to pursue different work. This kind of situation can be damaging to both you personally and your career.

While an incompetent boss can be annoying and frustrating, they aren't the worst kind of boss to have—unless they are nicely packaged with other shortcomings, like being a jerk or tossing you under the train for sport. Many times, you can make up for their shortcomings and Manage Up as they know innately that they lack many skills and knowledge. Don't let your frustration get in the way of managing the situation more effectively.

## The Bad Boss Who Undermines You

This type of Bad Boss may not be easily visible, which

makes your situation treacherous. It may take a while to realize what they are doing and the side effects.

The undermining boss may be doing things to subvert you behind your back without you ever realizing it when it takes place. They may or may not be consciously aware they are doing anything wrong. This person may seem to be somewhat normal without massive, obvious flaws like some of the other Bad Boss types. That's what makes them so bad.

This is not meant to make you paranoid, but simply to make you aware of the possibilities. You can work to repair any damage and you can take actions to prevent future erosion.

One of the problems with an undermining boss is that your response will be occurring after their deeds have been done.

Even if any damage has only slightly dented your work, the primary problem with this type of person is the loss of trust. Trust is a foundational basis of all relationships. When you can no longer trust another person, that affects your behavior from that point forward. This isn't positive or productive.

Let's look at the various ways a Bad Boss could undermine you:

- **TALKS ABOUT YOU TO OTHERS/SUBORDINATES.** While the boss does need to discuss people to others whom they are responsible to, I'm talking about the type of talk that is personal and inappropriate. This can range from disclosing confidential information about you, all the way to gossip. And it's not just what they are saying, it's whom they are saying it to. These conversations include your peers, which is quite wrong on the part of the Bad Boss. Even if your peers ignore what has been shared, chances are high that the conversation will get repeated. When this kind of behavior happens, it can be embarrassing and certainly serves no good intent.

- **CHANGES DIRECTION AND DOESN'T ACKNOWLEDGE DOING SO.** There are Bad Bosses out there who change direction almost daily. It's hard to keep ahead of them. Often, they don't realize they've changed direction. If this happens, they won't be communicating the change, because they may not realize anything different. At worst, they may get mad if you point out the change, which means you have that behavior to deal with as well. The impact on you is that you can't trust any directions from the Bad Boss because you know the potential for change is high and that there will be a subsequent loss of productivity as a result.

- **ELIMINATES CRITICAL RESOURCES.** You may wake up one day and find that your boss has removed resources you need to complete your work. They might not realize their decisions have that kind of effect. A loss of resources can mean you will miss a commitment and, therefore, your performance expectations.

As I mentioned, you won't find out about undermining behavior until after the fact and the damage to trust is done. It is important to emphasize that you don't want to ignore the behavior, because that will allow it to be repeated in the future. Often, the boss didn't realize what they did was an issue until it's too late. You want to have the perspective that what happened will be a learning experience for them. We can only hope.

What you can do?

- **SPEAK PRIVATELY WITH THE BOSS**. Don't set up a situation where they will be embarrassed by what they've done in front of others. If you do, that might go badly for you. Don't be emotional or overly confrontational. Instead, approach the dialogue as if you are trying to solve a problem.

- **IF THEY HAVE BREACHED YOUR CONFIDENCE WITH A PEER.** Be direct by what you were told or observed and ask for an explanation. Keep in mind that there may be two sides to the story, or a valid explanation. If it is a breach, explain the impact that behavior has on you but also on them (loss of trust). Be specific. Let them know this is not appropriate or acceptable and you expect to be treated better. Ask for their commitment to improve and discuss how rebuilding trust has to work moving forward.

- **ASK TO RECONCILE PREVIOUS DIRECTION WITH NEW DIRECTION.** There may be an explanation that bridges what sounds like conflicting or different direction. If the direction has changed, you need to indicate the impact of the change with specific comments such as how this affects timing, resources or productivity. Once you have outlined the impact, you need to ask for agreement on the expectations of your performance. Do not assume that just because the direction has changed that they've changed what their expectations are of you. You must ask.

- **HIGHLIGHT ANY IMPACTING SITUATION QUICKLY.** You don't want to assume the Bad Boss has knowingly eliminated resources unless you inform them. If you work the issue quickly, your actions may minimize any negative outcome for you. When you do have the conversation, be prepared to offer up solutions, as well as any changes, to your expected work.

As with any type of Bad Boss, trust is the thing that is damaged the most. You can't trust their treatment of you, their judgment, or decisions they make. Although trust can be rebuilt, it takes conscious effort for an extended period of time by the person who destroyed the trust. In the case of the Bad Boss, this isn't likely to happen.

Is it possible to work effectively with someone you don't trust? Only to a degree. Once trust is missing in the workplace, there will always be double-checking, validating, and questioning that slows down productive work.

# BAD BOSS STORY #4

## ANONYMOUS SOCIAL WORKER

"YOU MEAN LIKE that same boss who, because she's not around during the setup, or in the midst of an event, reverses critical decisions that are made in her absence? We've had about ten events this year. She's the last to arrive the day of the event and the first to leave. (I caught employees making bets on if she'd leave first at the last event.) And she takes off within hours before the event, or even during it. She leaves to pursue personal things. One of my favorites is when she is gone, comes in, checks around, delegates some tasks, and then leaves to get her hair or makeup done at a nearby salon. And yes, right before the meeting or event, she may take time out to change her clothes! Which is really not that bad, but once during one event she changed clothes three times. Yes, she did! (What's that all about?) Really, we're used to it, and we've learned to manage well around her. The hard part can be that she never checks in, even with new staff, to see if they have taken a break. And of course, she's hard pressed to lift a finger—can't damage her nails. The thing is, she thinks she's managing, but she's really directing, which works well when you're working with event professionals, but we are counselors, not event coordinators. But, who can stay mad at someone wearing Dior at a work party? We're all suffering, aren't we?

My solution has been to remember she's doing her best and to create events within the events, or jobs within the events, that keep me busy and off of her task list. I also practice meditation whenever I can on those days. One-minute meditations can bring miracles.

## My thoughts on Managing this Bad Boss:

Obviously, this Bad Boss is not a role model for good work ethics, communication, expectation setting, or delegation. The thing that makes this bad is she is gone so much and is unable to provide any useful, ongoing direction. While it's good that she is delegating, she isn't providing enough information for her group to execute to her expectations. As a result, they produce work that doesn't meet her expectations and makes the group unproductive. As well, what she is causing is a loss of trust that the work they do or the direction she provides won't be reversed.

I'd suggest this person do a few things to improve the situation:

- Ask her what activities she is working on that might involve assignment of work and any event dates. Do this routinely. This could provide a heads-up on possible activities that usually get assigned at the last minute and without advanced consultation.

- Ask for more operating parameters around delegated work in order to do a better job of completing assigned tasks when she is absent. This will help to avoid the need to redo the work. Consider using previous "re-worked" assignments as examples to help formulate more input from her about her expectations, then apply these going forward.

- Consider asking her if they can text or call her if she is going to be absent for more than an hour in order to clarify her direction on projects.

# You Hired *Who* to Be My Boss?
## OTHER MYSTERIES AND THINGS TO CONSIDER

I THINK IT'S IMPORTANT to answer once and for all: *How did the Bad Boss get the job?*

You and your peers are constantly scratching your heads wondering if the boss has compromising pictures of the CEO. How else could this insane person get the job? Particularly when they have no apparent skills, much less know anything about your area. This is a good question and I'm here to provide you with some insight. This insight is intended to not only explain this life mystery, but to shed light on your own professional growth plan.

Here are some of reasons for these horrific decisions:

- **THERE WASN'T A BETTER CANDIDATE.** You hear this with political candidates all the time. In the business setting, sometimes the big boss simply has no better choice and making no choice is worse than making a bad choice.

- They are valuable to the big boss. The big boss might be familiar with this person and find that they work together well. They may lack complete insight into how poorly the Bad Boss manages down, but their ability to manage up is superb. This happens a lot.

- **THEY ARE A "SUPER-DOER."** This is a phrase I personally coined. Often a person is great at something such as sales or business strategy. In order to reward them and create a growth path for them as a means of retaining all that great skill set, the big boss puts them in charge. They probably are encouraged to continue to do the work they are so famous for, completely bypassing any substantial leadership.

I had one of these bosses once and he was completely clueless and wanted to stay that way. I know, because I asked. He was the best salesman the company had and a very nice guy, which made his badness at least somewhat tolerable. He made bad decisions, couldn't manage, and wasn't around much because he was still making sales calls. At least when he was gone, us inmates ran the asylum and work went well.

- **THEY HAVE CHARISMA OR PERSONAL POWER.** You see this a lot. The person may know nothing, but what they say and how they say it sounds smooth as butter. This is a superficial person. Once you get into the trenches with them as your boss, they can't manage or do much of anything else. This person is a great figurehead, but provides nothing to you or your peers.

- **THEY FOOLED THEM.** This happens mostly with hires made from the outside. There is this concept known as "résumé drift." It's the idea that a résumé represents a person to be more experienced and skilled than they truly are. Some people can carry this into the interview and sound great . . . until they turn into your boss. It will take the big boss a while to figure out the deficiencies, and once they do, they may be reluctant to fix the problem.

- **THE BIG BOSS KNOWS BUT ISN'T WILLING TO DO ANYTHING.** Sometimes the big boss acquires your boss through organizational shuffling. Managing performance is difficult and many people are reluctant to make tough choices. The Bad Boss simply drifts along, making work-life miserable, and no one is going to do anything.

I'm sure there are a few bosses who got their job for other reasons, but I think this covers the majority. As I have said to those managers who reported to me: "You will be the single biggest factor in whether or not your people will like their job. Your job is to get the work done without taking a body count." If it was easy to be a good leader, we  wouldn't have so many books and workshops on how to be a good one.

## New Boss? New Career Opportunities

The one thing you can count on in business is nothing ever stays the same. That goes for the boss, too. Bosses come and go, even when your job remains in place. In some businesses, they come and go so fast they feel like a hit and run. While it would be nice to have some stability, it's not something you can count on. You can look at the boss turnover as a career growth opportunity.

When you get a new boss, the board is wiped clean and a new working relationship has yet to be developed. If your previous relationship was rocky or you performed some career-limiting moves, this gives you an opportunity to recreate who you are to that new person. Even if the new boss is someone you already know, you are both new in this work relationship and you have a chance to rethink how things will go. The key is to think about your next actions.

Here are some smart career moves when you get a new boss:

- **EDUCATE THEM ABOUT WHAT YOU DO.** You can't assume the new boss knows the details of who does what. They have a learning curve, so make sure you help them understand your job. Among the things you can share are your primary deliverables, results, current performance, what you are working on, and what you are slated to work on soon.

- **DON'T COMPARE THEM TO THE PREVIOUS BOSS.** They will resent the comparison. They will also more than likely want to do things differently than how they were done. Even if the previous boss was a felon, don't pass on bad gossip to the new boss. The assumption is that if you freely share your opinion of that person, you will do the same thing with the new person as well. This behavior doesn't win points.

- **TIME YOUR REQUESTS AND DECISION-MAKING.** If you hit up a new boss for things like time off, vacations, raises or even process decisions you will come off as un-savvy. Obviously, if there is a big decision that affects the business, you shouldn't hold off, but be prepared with a recommendation for a decision, your rationale, and any critical timing information. Aside from situations like that, allow the learning curve to take place and bring topics to them in small doses.

- **TIME TO SHINE.** If you were doing less than stellar under the previous boss, now is the time to hit the reset button on your performance. If you can make strides in the areas of improvement now that you are with a new boss, this boss will trust their own observations of you more than anything passed on to them. If you need to get a mentor to help you understand what you should be doing, now is the time to get that person lined up. It doesn't have to be public knowledge that you have a mentor. A mentor can help your career whether it is how to navigate the political landscape or how to improve your performance.

- **LEARN YOUR NEW BOSS.** Some people think a new boss will yearn to hear all their pent-up improvement suggestions. Like all people, the boss will only want advice if they ask for it. Learn how your new boss likes to learn and take in new information. How do they want to run the department? Do they want loads of detail, or only top-level information? Again, you can't make assumptions about the new boss based on history. Ask them questions about what they will want to know from you and then deliver.

- **BE READY FOR CHANGE.** Even when a peer ascends to the throne, things will change. Every boss will tweak things, sometimes making huge changes and other times only minor ones. Your willingness to actively embrace those changes can mean the difference between a successful working relationship and career or being advised that perhaps you'd fit better somewhere else.

Just like starting fresh with a new job, getting a new boss can be a great time to start over again and create real career momentum. You don't have to hang on to your old stories. You can rewrite your career each and every time a new boss comes along.

## What You Can Learn from the Boss's Favorite Suck-Up

I probably know what you're thinking. The thought of an office suck-up is disgusting, and you certainly don't want to learn from them. Your personal ethics prevent you from finding anything redeemable about this person. You may even think this person has caused you problems in the eyes of your boss. How on earth could this be someone to learn from?

Before thinking the boss can't see what is taking place right under their nose, consider how their job works and why this might be a good thing:

- **PERFORMANCE.** The boss is in charge of the performance of a number of people. Way too many people think a boss should "just know" what they do and how they do it. Wrong. The boss has to figure out a way to determine your performance. When an employee makes that easy for the boss, they gain favor. The suck-up is busy ensuring they keep the boss informed of their activities and obviously can put a "spin" on their work in the process. With or without biased input, when an employee is forthcoming with work insight, they score points. Those are points you could be obtaining as well.

- **BE TRANSPARENT.** When you act as an open book

about what you are doing, especially with the boss, you are building a bank account of trust. While that may not be 100% true for the suck-up employee, if the majority of what they are doing is transparent and easy for the boss to see, the trust goes up considerably.

- **FIRST TO SET THE STANDARD.** All too often the suck-up is the one to communicate first and frequently. When this is done, it quickly turns into a standard in the mind of the boss. Maybe it shouldn't be, but that happens. If the suck-up's point of view and standards are different than yours, you can become a problem. You may know your work is better, but your work isn't like the suck-up's. This means you could be at risk of losing your job because your work is out of alignment with what the suck-up does. Don't think that hunkering down in your office is going to win you any points or prevent the dreaded "performance discussion." Get yourself into the boss's office and start engaging them in your work. This will help keep the boss balanced on how they see each person in the group.

- **BRANDING.** Your brand is always showing even if you don't pay attention to it. The suck-up wants to be viewed positively. They clearly are ensuring the boss knows their brand and the value associated with that brand. You may not agree, but whose opinion matters? You can build your brand value easily by being clear on what you bring to the party, then finding ways of reinforcing that value. We are the only one to self-promote, and if you're concerned about being icky when you do, find a way to do so that feels authentic to you.

- **ASSET.** The suck-up may be considered an asset because they are spending time learning about the demands being made on the boss. By doing that, they can find ways of directly helping the boss without much additional workload. All managers want their employees to perform, but when an employee goes out of their way to be helpful, they are not just a good employee but also an asset. When a manager has an asset—they hold on to that asset. Keep that in mind every day.

There are always things we can learn from others, even people we don't like or respect. Keep your mind open and keep alert to possibilities. You may find some gold nuggets in the process.

## How to Disagree with the Boss

Disagreeing with other people, without taking a body count or courting disaster, is something most people try to avoid as much as possible. Nevertheless, we recognize that we can't always agree with everything that comes our way—even if it comes from the boss. Many of us think that disagreement with the boss is one of those career-limiting moves to be avoided as all costs. Think again.

Most managers want to think they've hired brilliant people who can think and act well on the company's behalf. That includes not letting them or anyone else drive off a metaphorical cliff. That means you are being paid to use your brain AND mouth. The diversity that takes place in the workplace isn't just about race or religion: it's about ideas, perspectives, and insight. If you are truly engaging in what is taking place at work, it's not possible to agree with the boss 100% of the time.

You can disagree with the boss and make that disagreement a win-win for both of you. You can win because you can make it career enhancing. The boss can win because they will come off as an engaging manager and get a much better end result.

Here are some ways to turn disagreement into a great thing for your career:

- **DISAGREE, BUT DON'T BE DISAGREEABLE.** When something strikes you as wrong or out of line, keep your emotions in check. No one, especially the boss, will appreciate an emotionally-charged rebuttal. People tend to mirror each other's energy level; and if you turn red and flap your arms, your behavior will be met with equal intensity.

- **MAKE YOUR DISAGREEMENTS COUNT.** Make sure your disagreements aren't an ongoing, daily thing. It can try the most patient leader if they know they can count on you to disagree with something. At that point, you're just a pain.

I had an intense woman work for me for a few years. She had a good head on her shoulders . . . which was maybe her only redeeming quality. She also got overly  intense with me or anyone else if she disagreed—to the point that it came off as outrage and moral indignation. It became tiring and not fun to work with her, which is never a good thing. Needless to say, I didn't miss her when I took my next position.

- **DON'T TAKE THINGS PERSONALLY.** The conversation will go much better if you are addressing the issue or topic and not making your disagreement about the person—in this case, your boss.

- **BE CLEAR ABOUT WHAT YOU DON'T AGREE WITH.** If you can't articulate what is troubling you, wait until you can be clear. If you can't be clear, you will not be able to have a conversation that will make any sense to the recipient. A confusing conversation will not leave a great impression.

- **OFFER ALTERNATIVES.** Nothing falls flatter than squashing an idea only to have nothing to replace it with. If you can't think up a better idea, then what good is the disagreement? Sure, you might not like the idea, but if you can't come up with something else, then go with what you have. You have to solve problems to be an asset.

- **KEEP THINGS PRIVATE.** Depending on the setting and issue, you may need to take your disagreement to a private setting with your boss. This allows you to have a discussion and keep both of you looking good to the rest of the office. You never want to embarrass the boss. If you do, they will remember much too long. They will appreciate your sensitivity and professionalism when you have the insight to know when it's time to have a private discussion.

- **SEEK TO UNDERSTAND.** Many conflicts and disagreements are rooted in a failure to communicate and understand the other person. When something does arise that doesn't hit you right, ask questions and gain clarity. You may discover you agree after all. Doing this will also help you avoid discomfort.

- **NO ONE LIKES "YES" PEOPLE.** This is more than simply sucking up to the boss. This is agreeing with the boss at the cost of your character, values and career. You might think it will enhance your career, but it will backfire against you as the higher-ups see that your contributions are limited. Just because the boss hasn't said anything about "yes" people, doesn't mean they can't tell or aren't disgusted by that kind of behavior.

- **DISAGREE AND COMMIT.** The biggest issue managers have when employees disagree is their becoming insubordinate and undermining efforts. If you have followed all of these steps and you still have disagreement,  then it's time for you to disagree and commit yourself to whatever is being proposed. After all, the idea or direction might really work out well. Your manager will think you are truly a professional if you can work through your disagreement, offer solutions, and be able to "get on board."

Certainly, out there in the universe there are managers with fragile egos who can't tolerate anyone disagreeing with their mandates or directions. This type of manager will only get just so far in their career. Anytime you limit the free flow of thought and contribution, you limit the possibilities. You need to screen for these people in your job search. If you wind up with a boss like that, you should consider a different group or job.

Fortunately, most managers enjoy discussion and debate as a means of developing great ideas and direction. They understand that disagreement is part of the process.

## What To Do When Everyone Loves The Boss But You

Just because the boss has a following at work doesn't mean you are going to be a follower. You have no idea why your opinion is so different than your peers and that has you scratching your head. The deal is, when you can't stand the boss, it can make your work life miserable. The great thing about this situation is that you have people around you who see this person differently. All is not lost. You could very likely change your reactions to the boss. The key to this situation is change. Change can be a tough thing to do, particularly when you're convinced of all the boss's flaws and look for daily confirmation that you're right. We get very invested in our attitudes about people. We think that the boss is the one who needs to change. The reason why it's got to be you to change is because you are the only one in this equation that you can control.

Here are some tips for how you can change and improve how you view the boss:

- **GET CLEAR ABOUT WHAT DOESN'T WORK FOR YOU.** Spend some time understanding what about the boss's behavior doesn't work for you. This must be actual, observable action's the boss exhibits. All too often when we don't like someone, we start focusing on our beliefs about this person instead of their true behavior. Spending time getting down to something real is important to solving this problem.

- **DISCOVER OTHER VIEWPOINTS.** Sit down with various people in your group to gain an understanding of what attributes they see in the boss. Ask enough questions so you can hear examples of what they see and how they see the positive qualities in the boss.

- **TEST THE ISSUES YOU FEEL CLEAR ABOUT.** With a select handful of people, you can speak about the boss's attributes. Ask them about observable behaviors. Don't try to convince them they shouldn't like the boss, simply ask them if they see the same things you do. You may find these issues are not considered a big deal, or that they are of minor concern compared to the positives they see. We all have warts, so it could be that you are placing much more importance on flaws than is necessary.

- **GET BETTER ACQUAINTED WITH THE BOSS.** Most people tend to avoid a person they don't like. This does nothing to help you improve your perspectives about this person. Spend time getting to know the boss and the positive attributes you have learned about from your peers. Often when we get to know a person better the flaws we once saw become minimized.

- **CHECK YOUR REACTIONS.** You could be blowing things out of proportion. If that is true for this boss, it could be how you react on many things. As a general rule, there are few things that warrant strong, negative feelings. If you have other unlikeable people in your work life, you may need to seek help so you can put things in proper proportion. Even if your reactions are mostly narrowed down to the boss, chances are still high that you are over reacting and need to counsel yourself to rethink what and how you react.

- **GET OVER YOURSELF.** Don't get so invested in the idea that your boss is bad that you can't change your viewpoint. I have seen people who didn't like the boss's personality and work style to the point that it became their own daily obsession.

I know a woman who hated her boss simply because he wasn't as effusive as she was. He didn't greet her warmly when she came to work and would occasionally simply observe her while she served the customers. As near as I could tell, he was an introvert. When I started explaining how some of what she wanted from this person was not going to be forthcoming because of his personality, she simply refused to understand. She said there was no excuse for not being friendlier, personality or not! I kept at it, trying to explain that what she was asking was like asking a right-handed person to start using only their left hand. I suggested she try engaging her boss instead of expecting him to engage with her. Before I continue to give you too much detail, the bottom-line is that she had one yardstick for goodness and it was hers. No room for insight. No room for adjusting behavior. Her choice to lack empathy for personality differences meant she was choosing to be miserable.

I have seen this many times with people who fail to understand inherent personality differences with the boss. Just like the rest of us, bosses come in all varieties. Most of the time, our usual way of interacting with those differences will work. When that doesn't happen, we go to the dark place of "there's something wrong with this person" instead of considering it might be us, or think we need to adjust.

Working effectively with other personality types means you must adjust your approach if you want to get along, regardless if they are the boss or a co-worker. First, you have to get over yourself and realize that "soft skills" are how we interact with others. You can't use the same approach and same skills with everyone you meet. You adjust—and if you are really going to manage your Bad Boss the first thing you have to adjust is *your* thinking.

You may never turn into a fan of the boss. The clue that you can improve from where you are now is in the fact that your peers find value where you don't. You can learn from your peers and do a great deal to improve your view of this person. You're not compromising your values. You're working at gaining insight. This is worth the effort because you spend a lot of your life around the boss and it will improve your outlook.

## What to Do When Your Best Friend Becomes Your Boss

When you are in the workplace long enough, you accumulate work friends as meaningful to you as non-work friends. One thing about work friends is that you sometimes have situations arise that are difficult to effectively manage. One of those is when your best work friend becomes your boss. It's apt to happen sooner or later. I know some people make jokes that you've got it made, but you don't really have anything made. In fact, without some mature thought you could lose a friend permanently, or even put your job at risk.

Here are some things for you to consider:

- **YOUR RELATIONSHIP WILL AND SHOULD CHANGE.** Your friend can't be seen as playing favorites with you. Everyone has to feel they get an equal chance at assignments and opportunities. If your friend is at all mature, they will probably distance themselves—and you need to support that shift. You want to stay friendly, but a certain level of professional detachment is in order for you both.

- **DON'T ASK FOR FAVORS.** Go out of your way avoid compromising your friend's position. Granted, all people ask favors of the boss at some point, but make sure you wait a long time before making your requests.

- **CHECK IN ON YOUR PERFORMANCE.** Just because you are friends, doesn't mean they think you do a great job. Understand one role that your friend—now manager—plays is to assess your performance. I've worked with a number of work friends over the years whose performance I thought was marginal. I would have hated to have those people work for me, because I would have had to take action to spiff them up . . . and that isn't a fun process. It can damage a friendship.

- **SIT DOWN AND TALK ABOUT THIS CHANGE.** Rather than just make assumptions about each other, do both of you a favor and have a chat. It would be great for you to acknowledge they are the boss and let them know you can separate a personal and professional relationship. Open the door to have future conversations so you can both check in to see if you have each adjusted to your new roles and tweak anything that might not be working well.

- **DON'T SHARE DETAILS WITH THE GROUP.** You might have personal and private knowledge of your friend that should never be shared. Sharing their information might make you momentarily feel like you have an inside track, but this won't be worth it in the long run. The deal is, almost everything gets back to the boss. Being a gossip isn't a tag you want. You will do irreparable damage to the entire relationship if you have loose lips. Trust is an important value in both friendship and work relationships. It only takes one stupid act to blow that trust.

- **DON'T TAKE THINGS PERSONALLY.** The boss (your friend) has new responsibilities, which means they could make decisions you might not like. More than likely, those kinds of decisions will be driven by business reasons, so don't make your first assumption that it's about you. If you have an issue, talk privately so you can problem-solve, just like you would with your previous boss.

- **IT'S OKAY TO ACT AS COUNSEL.** Because of your trusted relationship, your friend may seek you out for insight or to bounce ideas around. As mentioned previously, don't share these conversations with others. You may need to also ensure that you don't share too much information about your peers to your boss/friend, unless you know they can handle the information appropriately.

- **ACT PROFESSIONALLY.** The best advice for how you want to proceed is to act professionally. Keep business and personal relationships separate.

Who knows, you could become the boss of your best friend. You never know how things will work out, but the main thing you want to accomplish is to continue working effectively and maintaining a good working relationship.

# BAD BOSS STORY #5

### DR. LAWRENCE CLARK, PHD
### "THE COMMUNICATION LEADER"

I WAS TEACHING AT A college and I helped usher in the idea of doing a community event showcasing various work by faculty and students on our campus. This series of events happened as frequently as 10-12 times per semester. Sometimes it was a musical performance or a lecture by a professor or a student discussing a paper or doing a poetry or fiction reading. The range of topics was vast, and the series became very popular.

I was the one who coordinated the event and publicity, even though it wasn't an official part of my job. I volunteered to do this extra work because it helped the school and was good for community relations. After a few successful years of coordinating this event, a new boss arrived who was a couple of levels above me. Almost immediately, he began questioning every detail of this event, disparaging the topics and indicating his lack of approval. As time went on, this Bad Boss wanted to approve all the publicity for these events as well as each person who would be scheduled to perform or give a lecture or reading.

This created a huge burden on my volunteer time and eroded my motivation to keep working on it. I stopped coordinating the event and soon after left the university entirely, not just because of this situation, but due to a host of other poor management decisions by this Bad Boss.

## My thoughts about this Bad Boss:

Have we ever heard of not fixing something that wasn't broken? Like so many managers new to their position, there always seems to be a compulsion to change things. The thing that separates a good manager from a bad one is when they make changes simply for the sake of changing. The boss failed to understand something that was working well and should have been left as is. The entire school would have worked better if they were focusing on improving things that really needed improvement. This employee rolled with the punches that the Bad Boss launched and responded to the new levels of approval and scrutiny until it became unproductive. He stopped coordinating the community event, which was probably the best option. He could have had a discussion with this boss to come to an understanding of the goals for such an activity. This could have allowed them both to see if there could be a possible agreement going forward to return the coordination back to being productive and enjoyable. I do advocate this course of action before pulling the plug, but in light of other poor management performed by this Bad Boss, it was the best action.

# BONUS:
# MORE BAD BOSS STORIES
(AND THOUGHTS FROM DOROTHY)

## DR. LAWRENCE CLARK, PHD
## THE COMMUNICATION LEADER

MY FIRST "BAD BOSS" was with the first job I ever had. I was a fifteen-year-old, working as a dishwasher in one of two restaurants in my tiny hometown. I loved my job! I was earning money, got be around food and cooking (which I acquired a great love for) and worked with great people. It was a good job—at least when the boss wasn't around!

The work kept me on my toes, as I had to keep up with both the dinner dishes brought in by the wait staff and also the pots and pans with lots of burnt-on food from the chef. The process was to first use a strong spray hose to remove the food. If that didn't work, the next step was to use a wooden bristle brush to scrub the food off before putting the dishes in a big, restaurant-style dishwasher.

The process went well until my boss, a German immigrant with a thick accent, would come and check on me. He had a specific way he wanted the scrub brush to be held when I was removing food that had been stuck to the plates. It didn't matter to the boss that I was accomplishing the end result of having sparkling clean dishes available for the customers. What mattered more to him was how I held the darned scrub brush.

The problem was that the way the boss wanted me to hold the brush wouldn't work for me because I was left-handed and holding it the way he wanted me to was awkward and hurt my wrist. When he would leave, I would go back to holding the brush the way it worked best for me.

It became an obsession with the boss to see if he could catch me holding the brush the wrong way. When he did catch me, he would grab the brush out of my hand, shove me around, and yell at me with his thick German accent. On the one hand, it was almost comical, as he reminded me of Colonel Clink from the TV show "Hogan's Heroes." On the other hand, I took pride in my work, and it actually hurt my feelings that he didn't notice all the other good things I was doing, but instead chose to focus on this one irrelevant detail. This could make a good night at work go bad immediately, but since I enjoyed working with the rest of the crew, and since I lived in a small town with few other opportunities for part-time work, I held onto that job for quite a while until something better eventually came along.

## My thoughts on this Bad Boss:

As a fifteen-year-old, few skills existed for this poor kid to help him improve his situation. If he had mastered confrontation and negotiation skills, he could have appealed to the logic of this Bad Boss using those skills. As it was, this young employee stuck it out, and that's about the best he could have done.

This is an example of when a boss has lost site of the goal. The fact that the dishes and pots were clean and available when they were needed was the goal, but the boss got lost in the process, resorting to micromanaging instead of trusting his employee to get the work done.

Additionally, his interactions with the young employee were obviously over-the-top. It was abusive and demeaning for the employer to treat his employee with "manhandling" and yelling. The boss probably saw this young man as unempowered and took more liberties to vent his own personal stress, knowing he wouldn't be stopped. Unfortunately, people will do this if they think they can get by with it. An adult with even a modest amount of self-respect and conflict skills would have put that behavior to a stop.

## DR. LAWRENCE CLARK, PHD
## THE COMMUNICATION LEADER

I WAS WORKING AS a technical writer for a high-tech company. The equipment my company manufactured cost millions of dollars and was intricate and potentially dangerous. The process the machines used included a poisonous gas that could kill someone before they even realized there was a leak. My job was to write instructions for the people who operated these one-of-a-kind machines so they could successfully and safely operate and maintain them. To accomplish my work, I would often spend time with the people who built and operated the equipment so I could translate the correct procedures into written instructions. Just to give you an idea of how involved these instructions were, we produced up to fifteen manuals per piece of equipment, each with about 400-500 pages of instructions. After spending some time with the machine's installers, operators, and maintenance workers, I learned that almost no one had read any of the instruction manuals. I came up with the idea of preparing a video for each corresponding task that could be accessed at the appropriate point through a touch-screen mounted on the side of the unit. The only problem was, I worked in the "technical writing" department, but the audio-video department was a separate group.

My boss did not want me spending time with the A/V department because producing my idea would make that department look good and his department look bad. For him, it was beside the point that it would keep the operators safe and the equipment working well.

To make matters worse, I was a senior-level technical writer with a PhD in communications and several years of experience producing technical materials, but my supervisor was ignoring my capabilities. For example, one morning he held a staff meeting and told our team he had decided that our manuals wasted too much paper. His idea was for us to go through each line of information in those lengthy manuals and remove spaces in order to shrink the text and subsequently paper. I spent the good part of three months counting and removing spaces in those manuals, wondering why I had invested all that money and all those years obtaining a higher education.

But that's not all, folks; it actually got worse. When the time came for my annual performance evaluation, I was marked as "medium" on productivity. I said I didn't understand how my work could be marked as anything short of excellent. The standard the boss set was for each team member to edit three chapters per week, and I was doing ten per week! Rather than concede the point, the boss responded that he expected that I could edit twenty per month. Of course, he had never articulated this expectation until that very moment.

Since I had signed a one-year contract with that company, it should go without saying that I didn't renew my contract. Yes, I was getting paid a great deal more in this position than I was previously making, so one would think the higher pay would be an incentive to stay. But I was miserable and was not being allowed to live up to my potential, so it didn't matter how much I was getting paid.

### My thoughts on this Bad Boss:

Although this boss wasn't yelling and berating this employee, his complete lack of using his highly-skilled  employee appropriately set the stage for a poor working environment. He failed to set performance expectations and communicate them. He failed to look at the bigger picture of the company's needs and goals. Instead, he pursued his own ego-driven agenda. Lastly, he failed to collaborate with his employees to solve problems and improve the output of his department. As a result, he came up with complete nonsense assignments.

This employee did the best he could with this boss. He offered suggestions for improvement, which were rejected. The employee confronted the boss with documented performance expectations, which was good to do even though it failed to change the mind of the Bad Boss.

This is a good illustration that pay is never as important as being respected and working well with the boss.

## AS TOLD BY A FORMER HR EXECUTIVE
## IN AN HIGH TECH/FORTUNE 500 COMPANY

"MANY OF THE POSITIONS in HR for large companies involve being assigned to support specific business groups, essentially giving you two leaders to be accountable to. This was my situation for most of my HR career. At one point, I worked for a woman who was a brilliant "up-and-comer" in the company. Even as brilliant as she was, she was unable to clearly articulate her expectations of work she assigned to her people.

Working for her often felt futile, as you would bring her the work you thought she wanted, but often she rejected it and demanded a rework. When that occurred, her ability to clarify her direction didn't improve. In fact, it became apparent her instructions were like a moving target, they would change from one interaction to the next. It was only after you had repeatedly brought her the same assignment in multiple revisions, that she would eventually find what she wanted. Whatever you provided was also met with scorn and intimidation.

Attempts to ask her clarifying questions were met with hostility and demeaning language. She tagged you as stupid and said she was "paying you to use your brain."

I came to realize her process. She was asking several people to do the same thing and was using the instruction and discussion as a means to help her further define what she wanted. That's what caused her directions to change from one time to the next. Never mind how unproductive and frustrating it was to be chasing after something that wasn't going to satisfy her, but also to be pelted with a barrage of berating language. Very motivational (not).

Others and myself came to realize the best way to self-manage the situation was to not react or start work on the first wave of input. We knew the direction would change and become more refined the more she had an opportunity to articulate her needs. It was also better to fail her by not having something to show her and being late than it was to anger her by delivering something she didn't want.

Part of the dysfunction of this leader was that she ruled by intimidation both up and down the food chain. Her intimidation was a combination of over-positioning the dire outcome of not aligning to her direction and a hefty reminder of how brilliant she was. The message became "if you're too stupid to agree, you will be responsible for a seriously bad outcome."

Eventually, this manager was shuffled to a position with less responsibility and people management.

### My thoughts on this Bad Boss:

This employee did a lot of the right things. She spent time trying to understand the dysfunction of her boss in order to minimize the negative effects. Once she understood how the boss worked, she optimized her approach to her assignments in order to reduce the abuse. This approach didn't entirely eliminate all bad encounters, but it reduced the number and intensity.

A manager who is unable to clearly define an outcome would do well to disclose the limitation to her staff and use this as an opportunity to create a think tank. A leader doesn't need to have all the answers and should call upon employees to generate ideas. Doing so enhances everyone's situation, including that of the leader. This Bad Boss missed the opportunity to inspire her staff through active collaboration.

## KRISTEN CLARK:
### CONFIDENCE COACH, AWARD-WINNING AUTHOR, EDITOR, PUBLISHER
www.AmericanMuttPress.com

### WORKED IN A FORTUNE 50 COMPANY

I WORKED FOR A woman who was new to her role. In her new role, she acquired a number of employees, including me. Very quickly, it became apparent she and I didn't mesh well. She was critical and judgmental, and wasn't accurate with her assessment of my work. It wasn't her opinion versus mine; it was that she was incorrect about the work. One of my personal values is to do my work with a high level of excellence and to have someone disparage my work was almost intolerable. I knew disagreeing with her or confronting her would only make matters worse, so I chose to rise above the environment she had created and not take it personally. I also decided to document examples of her inaccuracies to prove my point when necessary.

Despite her ongoing barrage of negativity, I thought it important to live in the integrity of my values. I didn't want to complain about her or be in a space of negativity.

At one point, she had the opportunity to reduce her headcount and my name had topped her list of people to get rid of. I could have taken the news badly, but decided otherwise.

I decided, instead, to immediately reach out to other managers in the company in search of a new position. Because I was a good employee and had a stellar reputation, I was able to secure a new position before becoming unemployed. Not only that, but the new position came with a promotion and a pay raise!

### My thoughts on this Bad Boss:

This woman did everything right. She self-managed well and did her best to stay positive. She had the courage to point out the inaccuracies of the work assessment, which is really a form of training of the manager. I'm sure even if this Bad Boss tried to ignore what was being shared, she learned something in the process.

Another thing I would like to point out. This manager worked in a huge, international company that had budgets for management training. More than likely, this Bad Boss had some training and, despite any training she received, she still had a tough time being a good leader to a superb employee. I think the public often thinks that Bad Bosses occur in small companies that are unable to afford management training. This story tells us that the Bad Boss can show up in any size company and continue to be bad, even with good training.

**KRISTEN CLARK:**
CONFIDENCE COACH, AWARD-WINNING AUTHOR,
EDITOR, PUBLISHER
www.AmericanMuttPress.com

WORKED IN A FORTUNE 50 COMPANY

M Y VP HAD WORKED for the company for a number of years and decided to retire. A man from Europe was promoted as his replacement, and his reputation for being difficult and brash preceded him. Upon our first encounter, my new boss requested that I always be upfront and direct with him.

Shortly after this, I found myself preparing him for a public event, and I had received a few concerns about how my new boss might come across to the scheduled American audience. I summoned up the courage to have a conversation with him about the feedback I received and offered to team up with him to make him successful. While he was stunned by both my boldness and directness, he developed a deep respect and trust for me from that point forward.

## My thoughts on this Bad Boss:

Keep in mind that your behavior can bring out the best or the worst in your boss. I'm sure the communication style of this VP was probably hard for many people to warm up to and, consequently be encouraged to be productive She did not personalize his style, but rather matched some level of directness, which worked for him.

# FINAL THOUGHTS

BAD BOSSES HAPPEN. This probably happens more than it should. If you take responsibility for your own career and personal happiness, you will find the ability to improve your situation when a Bad Boss takes over will go up tremendously. A Bad Boss has similarities to other people you will encounter in your career. Bad behavior is not the sole domain of management; you will find it in all places and in a variety of people. That fact alone makes it an imperative for you to have strategies you can use to optimize your work relationships.

If you have heard the term "soft skill", that is what you

are in the process of developing. When we talk about soft skills, we are talking about the ability to interact with people in effective ways. By now, you have to have gotten the point that one-size approaches to all people simply don't work. While your interactions will work with most people, most of the time, your strategies won't work with everyone. This is where you must trouble-shoot particular issues and figure out what changes YOU will make.

You will not have a successful career or a happy work-life if you hope the other person will change. You can't expect to change them. Being angry or frustrated isn't productive, nor does it change how things work. The one thing you have complete control over and can change is YOU.

I would like to leave you with one last thought. If you lead people now or anytime in the future, develop insight about your own behavior. I believe most Bad Bosses exist not because they wake up every day with the idea of making life miserable for you or anyone else. In fact, I think the Bad Boss lacks personal insight and thought about the impact of their behavior on others. Be the best possible leader you can be, as it not only makes you and those who work for you happier, you will have high-producing people. It doesn't get any better than that.

To a powerful career,

Dorothy

## WOULD YOU PLEASE REVIEW?

WOULD YOU BE so kind as to leave a book review? Authors' books have a much better chance at being successful when our readers share that they enjoyed reading the book and/or found it helpful . . . which I hope you did. If you could take a few minutes to leave a review, I'd appreciate it ever so much.

# VIDEO SERIES

Get Free Instant Access to Video series,

## "The 5 Most Common Ways Introverts Commit Career Self-Sabotage and How to Avoid Them"

These videos are designed to accelerate your results
with **Accelerate Your Career,**
and are my way of saying "thank you" for purchasing this book.

www.introvertwhisperer.com/career goals

# OTHER BOOKS FROM
# DOROTHY TANNAHILL-MORAN

## Career Mapping:
Planning Your Career on Purpose

## Easier Networking
for Introverts and the Socially Reluctant:
A 4-Step Guide That's Natural, Stress-Free and Gets Results

## Elevator Speeches
That Get Results

## Personal Branding:
A Simple Guide to Reinvent & Manage Your Brand
for Career Success

## ABOUT THE AUTHOR

**D**orothy **Tannahill-Moran** is *The Introvert Whisperer,* a leadership and career coach, author and speaker. Born an introvert, then shaped into a leader, she is a delightful fusion of unique, useful insight and rock-solid management expertise. As a Career Coach, she guides the reluctant toward better relationships with their boss and management, teaching introverts how to effectively collaborate with difficult people, navigate workplace culture and internal politics, and successfully network in a room filled with strangers. This is why Dorothy Tannhill-Moran is a sought-out and trusted advisor to corporate professionals and executives worldwide.

A graduate of Emporia State University with a Bachelor of Science in Education, Dorothy was recruited by the Kansas City School District to coordinate their Distributive Education program. Four years later, she was hired by Intel where she quickly rose through their ranks to senior-level management. With over twenty-one years supervising Intel's diverse staff mix, she coached, guided and trained others at all levels to achieve impressive careers, executive status, higher salaries, while gaining broad professional recognition. Twice Intel bestowed upon her their highest achievement award, spotlighting her outstanding accomplishments and the positive, long-lasting impact she made on their culture.

For more powerful career strategies, go to:
**www.introvertwhisperer.com**

Made in the USA
Middletown, DE
27 June 2019